REFORM AND RENEWAL
THOMAS CROMWELL AND THE COMMON WEAL

THE WILES LECTURES
GIVEN AT THE QUEEN'S UNIVERSITY BELFAST
1972

REFORM AND RENEWAL

THOMAS CROMWELL
AND THE COMMON WEAL

G.R.ELTON

CAMBRIDGE
AT THE UNIVERSITY PRESS
1973

Published by the Syndics of the Cambridge University Press
Bentley House, 200 Euston Road, London NW1 2DB
American Branch: 32 East 57th Street, New York, N.Y. 10022

Library of Congress Catalogue Card Number: 72–87180

ISBNs
0 521 20054 7 hard covers
0 521 09809 2 paperback

Printed in Great Britain by
Western Printing Services Ltd, Bristol

CONTENTS

PREFACE

The Wiles Lectures at The Queen's University, Belfast, have established themselves as the highlight of the academic historian's year. For once that much-abused term, symposium, may be properly used: *fratres, ergo bibamus – aquas doctrinae et aquam vitae*. I am deeply grateful to Mrs Janet Boyd (*fundatrici rerum*) and the trustees of the Wiles Foundation, as well as to the History Department at Queen's and especially Professor Michael Roberts, for inviting me to deliver the lectures in May 1972. I am for ever obliged to my colleagues at Queen's and to those friends who joined the occasion for providing so joyous a battle and so happy a peace. Especially I wish to thank Miss Helen Miller who, with her accustomed courtesy and familiar learning, saved me from some deplorable howlers. It alters a man's view of life to see how the comity of scholars may flourish even in a discommodity of nations.

The four lectures as delivered were compressed from the seven chapters of this book, and the necessity to fit things into a compass has imposed certain limitations upon the exploration of its theme. This is to be my last engagement with Thomas Cromwell, at least at book-length. In the quarter century since I first encountered that extraordinary man I have always wanted to study three sides of his multiple nature and work: the ruler of the state, the chief of police, and the promoter of reform. Though more can still be learned, that undertaking is now finished. The man who has at length emerged differs somewhat from the figure I first discerned those many years ago, though I remain convinced of one thing I believed about him from the first – his central position in the history of his time, the history of the Tudor century, and the history of England. But his cast of mind was less determinedly secular and less ruthlessly radical than I had once supposed. It was because he brought to the task of breaking-up and rebuilding firm principles of a spiritual renewal resting upon the truths of the past, as well as a clear-sighted conviction of the need for profound change, that his achievement reached so deep and lasted so well.

Clare College, Cambridge G.R.E.
May 1972

ABBREVIATIONS

I have modernized and standardized the spelling and punctuation of all citations, even where these are taken from printed books or modern editions. I believe that this practice makes access to the evidence much easier while depriving the reader of nothing of importance.

BM   British Museum

CUL   Cambridge University Library

E.E.T.S.   Early English Text Society

Ellis   Henry Ellis, ed., *Original Letters illustrative of English History*, 3 series, eleven vols. (London, 1824–1846)

LJ   *Journals of the House of Lords*

LP   *Letters and Papers, Foreign and Domestic, of the Reign of Henry VIII*, ed. J. S. Brewer, J. Gairdner, R. H. Brodie, 36 vols. (London, 1862–1932)

Merriman   Roger B. Merriman, *The Life and Letters of Thomas Cromwell*, 2 vols. (Oxford, 1902)

STC   *A Short-Title Catalogue of Books printed in England, Scotland and Ireland, and of English Books printed abroad, 1475–1640*, ed. A. W. Pollard and G. R. Redgrave (London, 1926)

StP   *State Papers of Henry VIII*, 11 vols. (London, 1830–1852)

TRP   *Tudor Royal Proclamations*, ed. Paul L. Hughes and James F. Larkin, 3 vols. (New Haven, 1964–1969)

Manuscripts cited without location are from the Public Record Office, London; the following classes have been used:

E 36	Exchequer, Treasury of the Receipt, Misc. Books
Req 2	Proceedings of the Court of Requests
SP 1	State Papers, Henry VIII
SP 2	the same, folio volumes
SP 6	the same, Theological Tracts
St Ch 2	Star Chamber Proceedings, Henry VIII

1

INTRODUCTION

In the past twenty years we have learned a good deal about the Tudor commonwealth – that concept of a responsible state committed to social, political and religious reform. Where once everything concentrated on the crisis years of Edward VI's reign, we are now taught to think of a philosophy repeatedly asserted and revised, a continuous attitude to public life making its effects felt among the agents of that life. And where earlier historians saw only statesmen and administrators reacting to the practical problems of the day, we have been shown the importance of intellectuals and writers. Humanism, often defined as Erasmianism, has usurped the place of leadership. Obscure thinkers are no longer obscure and somewhat more thoughtful. Commonwealth, Protestantism and Christian humanism have been jumbled together in a splendid porridge of reformist yearning; and I want to stress that in my opinion this cross-play of beliefs, weighing differently in different men, strikes much more convincingly than a distinction of categories which turns individuals into representatives of abstract ideas. Reform and reformation, as we have come to realize, were in the air in the early sixteenth century, in England as elsewhere; golden ages may have lain in the past, but that did not discourage men from supposing that they might manage, here and now, to approach more closely to that distant state of bliss. In England, this very general complex of ideas and aspirations gathered round the notion of the commonwealth, and we have learned increasingly what this meant and how pervasively it coloured all political thinking and practice.

Is there, then, any more to be said about problems that have attracted so much attention? Before I can answer that question, I propose to review briefly what our guides have told us. The pioneering study appeared in 1948: Gordon Zeeveld's investigation of the group that gathered round Reginald Pole at Padua and from there, returning to England, spread a new and practical gospel in the atmosphere of change produced by the early

Reformation.[1] Zeeveld's book was not only the first breakthrough on that front, after decades of work on the 'More group' and on the Edwardian reformers which implicitly denied any ideas to the Henrician reformers; in spite of a good deal more work since, it also remains the most remarkable, in part because Zeeveld recognized the importance of unprinted treatises. It was he who first drew attention to the impact of reformist humanism on the generation after Erasmus and More, who demonstrated that programmes and ideas played their part in the politics of the Henrician Reformation, and who plotted the contacts between Thomas Cromwell and the intellectuals. All these familiar commonplaces of today were new in 1948.

While Zeeveld made real sense of the proposition that his writers must be understood as involved in affairs, the next book on those themes retreated into a more conventional form of the history of ideas. The title of Fritz Caspari's study of the educational ideals propounded by four leading Tudor humanists made one hope for an analysis of social programmes which did not emerge.[2] The book has little relevance to our present purposes, except that it, too, demonstrated the English humanists' participation in a European complex of discussions – and except that people still cite it. Stanford Lehmberg's study of Sir Thomas Elyot brought a fuller understanding of one thinker, but it did not investigate the general intellectual society of the time: which is the less surprising because Elyot, though something of a friend of Cromwell's back to Wolsey's day, deliberately withdrew from public life into the study, and in consequence exercised little influence or none.[3] Elyot, who was quite a considerable writer, appears to have opted out of the chance grasped with both hands by Thomas Starkey; he demonstrated that some sympathy with the religious reforms of that administration was required before a man could hope to assist it in other ways.

It was not until 1965 that the questions asked by Zeeveld were taken up once more, in Arthur Ferguson's massive study of the

---

[1] W. Gordon Zeeveld, *Foundations of Tudor Policy* (Cambridge, Mass., 1948).
[2] F. Caspari, *Humanism and the Social Order in Tudor England* (Chicago, 1954).
[3] Stanford E. Lehmberg, *Sir Thomas Elyot, Tudor Humanist* (Austin, Texas, 1960).

main attitudes displayed by those second-rank thinkers.[4] Where
Zeeveld had concentrated on an identifiable group, living and
working together, and on arguments about the nature of political
society, Ferguson tried to range over two centuries and to demonstrate that the influence of Italian humanism, joined to a native
preoccupation with the practical problems of society, produced a
peculiarly English devotion to economic and social reform which,
after the shock of Henry VIII's break with Rome, erupted from
the study into the counsels of princes. He, too, emphasized the
part played by Cromwell in organizing the services of those
learned advisers. This type of investigation culminated, in the
same year, in James McConica's attempt to accommodate virtually every rational discussion of social, religious and political
problems in England from the mid-twenties to the mid-fifties
under the banner of Erasmianism.[5] Whatever one may think of
that label, McConica greatly advanced our understanding of the
body of ideas shared by these people, of their interaction with
the politicians, and especially of the manner in which the printing
press helped them to announce themselves. He also gave shape
to the earlier gropings after a chronological pattern by tracking
the migration of his Erasmian policy-makers and advisers from
one group to another – from Wolsey to Cromwell to Catherine
Parr to Somerset and the commonwealth-men traditionally so
called. This pattern also underlies the last significant contribution
to the discussion, Whitney Jones's analysis of the manner in
which the thinkers of those thirty years reacted to the impact of
events around them – the events of 'the social and economic
developments of mid-Tudor England'.[6] It is not without significance for a full evaluation of all this scholarship that Jones was
the first writer to break what had become an American monopoly,
and a monopoly of people brought up in the American tradition
of intellectual history at that.[7]

---

[4] Arthur B. Ferguson, *The Articulate Citizen and the English Renaissance*
(Durham, N.C., 1965).
[5] James K. McConica, *English Humanists and Reformation Politics under
Henry VIII and Edward VI* (Oxford, 1965).
[6] W. R. D. Jones, *The Tudor Commonwealth 1529–1559* (London, 1970).
[7] There have, of course, been other contributions of less significance in the
present context, and there is the whole complex of writings around
Thomas More and his *Utopia*, but it should be noted that the most famous
book of the early sixteenth century has no identifiable bearing on reformist
programmes after 1530.

This massive production, overlapping here and there but in general sufficiently diverse to indicate the remarkable fertility of the topic, has accounted for a variety of matters. We need not again investigate the derivation of *via media* concepts in the English Church, of practical interests among humanist thinkers, or of Erasmian notions of reform in every nook and cranny. In fact, the body of ideas as such needs at this time no further study, the more so because in itself it is far from remarkable. These Tudor writers were troubled by the state of the world, by its lack of honest spirituality and by social deficiencies, and they brought to their task of propounding reform some very simple basic ideas concerning the political perfectability of man's condition and a naïvely sanguine trust in the power of edicts to make men better. They were in all respects quite typical examples of 'social engineers'. Specific proposals circle round recurring themes: a cleaner Church, a more practical Christianity, the positive control of greed and selfishness, the greatness of England. Radical reformers are rarely very deep thinkers: deep thought about the human condition tends to promote pessimism and despair. What is worthy of notice (as all our authors have recognized) is those intellectuals' determination – a novel determination – to turn disapproval of the present and trust in reform into practical channels.

To indicate the relative simplicity of the ideals held by these writers is not to criticize the scholars who have given us such full expositions of that simplicity. If they may be criticized it is rather on two different grounds: one, a tendency to over-schematize things, and two, a surprising unwillingness to follow the thinkers into the public arena where they themselves wished to be. These are two characteristic pitfalls in the path trodden by historians of ideas, and in this case they do seem to me to hinder a correct understanding of what actually went on.

An excessive addiction to pattern-making is particularly marked in McConica's book; Ferguson falls victim to it to a lesser extent; Zeeveld, who writes as though he was unaware of the profound transformation in historical thinking he was initiating, has almost none of it. Ferguson probably over-labours his distinction between lamenting moralists and buoyantly reformist activists, though there is real insight in a classification which links the change with the Reformation. Thomas More, in *Utopia*, made

no proposals: he diagnosed ills and placed his remedies in the
fictional realm of the unattainable. Starkey, on the other hand,
tried to prescribe specifically for the actual realm of England.
But McConica's pursuit of Erasmus really distorts. When Cromwell's efforts are described as 'official Erasmianism' – that
Erasmianism which can be traced active in Wolsey's household
and allegedly entered politics with More's elevation to the
chancellorship – fundamental changes are obscured. The commonplaces of Erasmus' social thought were shared by most reformers:
they had to be because they were so commonplace. No doubt,
many of the younger humanists had read Erasmus though they
virtually never cite him; when they do, they do not use him for
ideas on the common weal.[8] What evidence is there that Pole's
Paduan circle attached themselves to an international Erasmianism? Less humanist writers – men like Clement Armstrong or
Christopher St German – showed even less of that godlike influence; yet this did not prevent them from proposing reforms
marked by similar 'Christian humanist' principles.[9] By the 1530's
Erasmus himself had ceased to provide new ideas, especially on
society, and his general reputation was much reduced. Of course,
Erasmus carried influence. I do not mean to deny his wide and
frequent effect upon all students and especially the aid and comfort he gave to religious reformers of whose ultimate ends he
often disapproved; but to order all that was written – worse, all
that was done – under that single device is to obscure the history
of events by hiding it behind a misleadingly comprehensive
generalization.

Another form of the excessive scheme, very relevant here,
afflicts Jones. True, he only follows doctrine in organizing all his
material under the theme of the 'Tudor commonwealth', but in
doing so he perpetuates a linguistic confusion. There are two
quite distinct meanings to the word, according as to whether it is
a compound noun or a noun qualified by an adjective. In the first
form it is used, occasionally, in the modern sense, to denote a

---

[8] Richard Morison once called Erasmus 'the greatest learned man of our
time', but though he did so in a book concerned with the social order he
used him only to quote some extravagant praise of Henry VIII (*A Remedy
for Sedition* [1536], sig. F iii–iv).
[9] Armstrong's manuscript treatise on the true Church and its function in
society is thoroughly evangelical but absolutely not Erasmian (SP 6/11,
fos. 103–33 [*LP* vi. 416]).

political structure. Thus Elyot starts off his *Governour* with a long and very pedantic disquisition on the term which, he says, has been used to translate the Latin *res publica* (itself, of course, capable of a similar double usage). He concludes that the translation is wrong: *res publica* should be rendered 'public weal', while commonwealth should be translated into Latin as *res plebeia*.[10] This is an absurdity, but an enlightening one. To Elyot, the 'commonalty. . . signifieth only the multitude wherein be contained the base and vulgar inhabitants not advanced to any honour and dignity';[11] his snob's commonwealth does not comprehend the concerns of the ruling classes. Clearly, therefore, he does not really regard the term as a description of the realm of England, the sense in which modern historians have taken it, and incidentally the sense canonized by the Rump Parliament. And indeed it is not easy to find people in the sixteenth century who did treat the word simply as though it described the nation in its temporal aspect. Richard Morison defined 'a common wealth' as 'a certain number of cities, towns, shires that all agree upon one law and one head', and throughout his book he used it to denote what the nineteenth century called the organic state.[12] But such occasional usage is rivalled by the more usual one which speaks of the common weal or wealth as the welfare, the well-being, of all members of the community (or of the lower orders only, according to Elyot). When a pamphleteer heads his treatise with the title, 'How the common people may be set to work: an order of a commonwealth',[13] he does not mean that he is about to set out the description of a polity or state, but that his proposals are designed to assist general social improvement. It is in this second sense that the term is just about always used in the statutes of the time. A certain country gentleman neatly exemplified the un-

---

[10] Thomas Elyot, *The Boke named the Governour*, ed. H. H. S. Croft (1883), i. 1–3.

[11] Ibid. 2. Possibly Elyot's influence may be found in the occasional attempts to evade the distinction by applying both adjectives. Thus a proposal to exempt schoolmasters from the payment of first fruits speaks of them as being 'necessary to the continuance of a public or a common wealth' (SP 1/104, fo. 152 [*LP* x. 1092]).

[12] *A Remedy for Sedition* pleads repeatedly that a true commonwealth, 'like a body', is a structure of all classes and kinds of people; when Morison asks, 'how can there be any commonwealth where he that is wealthiest is most like to come to woe?', he implicitly refutes Elyot's distinction.

[13] SP 1/242, fo. 126 (*LP Add.* 1382[1]).

conscious dilemma when he referred to 'this part of the common-weal' committed to himself and his fellow justices, meaning evidently a part of the realm, and then went on to cite a phrase from a royal circular about the King's 'loving mind to the common weal of this realm', where the term means the general advantage.[14] Though Tudor writers could employ 'common-wealth' to designate the realm – minus the King (and the clergy?) – they more usually meant by it 'that which will benefit the nation' or 'a matter of common benefit'. They do not, therefore, discuss and promote 'the commonwealth' so much as 'the common weal', a distinction which removes the party label of commonwealth-men which historians have stuck onto all these social reformers. Alternatively, commonwealth-men means simply all the social reformers (since there was only one school of thought on the subject), but either way nothing is gained and something is obscured by the habit of turning an obvious commonplace ('we seek the good of all') into an intellectual concept.[15]

If excessive schematization has landed us with intellectual parties – Erasmians or commonwealth-men – where in reality we have no more than like-minded troubled individuals with com-plaints about different aspects of society, failure to look beyond the complaints and prescriptions has obscured the activities of governments and the reality of the relations between thinkers and actors. None of the historians I have reviewed here has attempted a systematic study of the way in which articulate pro-test and intellectual remedy-mongering may have percolated into statutes and proclamations; none is really concerned with the mechanism of translating aspiration into achievement. This is not to blame them – they had enough to do – but it shows what still needs doing. Even Jones, who starts off with hints that he will attend to such questions and does list statutes supposedly related to reformist movements, soon is back with classifying writers and

---

[14] SP 1/241, fo. 110 (*LP Add.* 1241).

[15] Ferguson's discussion of 'the commonweal and the sense of change' (*Articulate Citizen*, ch. 13) also suffers from this failure to distinguish. 'The Tudor commonwealth,' he says, 'was a profoundly conservative ideal' (p. 366). It could be so in the hands of writers who treated the commonwealth as a single noun; the far greater number who thought they were speaking of general welfare could be conservative or radical about it as the remediable deficiencies in question might dictate.

writings, with extracting comment or ideas on topics ordered by himself, and with at most supposing that whatsoever was done was somehow a product of the 'movement' he discerns. Of course, the links between books and laws are always hard to trace. We know that a man like Thomas Starkey offered himself expressly as an adviser to the policy-makers; we have some exchange of views between him and Cromwell, and within the circle that surrounded both of them; yet even in his case direct effects are hard to prove, though some quite powerful probabilities emerge.[16] Yet if the place of these thinkers is to be understood, their ambition to affect real life should at least be investigated.

I offer these criticisms in no carping spirit. The achievements of men who have laboured through some extremely tedious and highly repetitive materials in order to uncover a whole generation of purposeful thinkers are exciting and command both the highest respect and that gratitude which springs from a realization that this, at least, is work one will not have to do oneself. It is because I still need to answer the question whether anything further can be done that I have ventured to stress the weaknesses in the case as stated hitherto. For it is into those gaps that I propose to wriggle. I do not and cannot claim to fill them; but I can try to look at the reality of a government in action for a purpose which we know was also being propounded by systematic thinkers. Not Erasmian government, not commonwealth government, not the government of proposals only; but the work of a markedly reformist government, and whether what it did reflected the existence of those advocates of reform. All our historians have, one way or another, put up signposts which I should like to follow: signposts pointing towards the statute book, towards executive action, towards (especially) the era of Thomas Cromwell as a time when thought yielded results in deeds. In short, I am about to undertake a case study both to test and to fill out our existing theories about the early-Tudor commonwealth, and I propose to start the enquiry by looking at the man who has been seen as both the organizer and the agent of the intellectuals.

[16] G. R. Elton, 'Reform by Statute: Thomas Starkey's *Dialogue* and Thomas Cromwell's Policy,' *Proceedings of the British Academy*, liv (1968), 165–188; and cf. below, pp. 46–55.

2

THOMAS CROMWELL

All the experts are agreed that the years of Thomas Cromwell's administration marked an important stage in the thought and practice of social reform, but they are less unanimous or even clear about the role played by the minister himself. Zeeveld recognized his control of the propaganda machine and the intellectuals, but felt that Cromwell's own thought remained strictly pragmatic and concerned with expediency; he could in no way regard him as a radical anxious to remake the commonwealth.[1] Ferguson, sure that men of the new learning were employed solely for the purpose of serving the King's political aims, echoed this view.[2] McConica, though willing to speak of Cromwell's 'astute genius', saw him only in the role of a recruiter; he did not regard him as a man who contributed ideas and purposes of his own.[3] And while Jones admitted that the Cromwellian group manifested their concern with social progress, he doubted the minister's own commitment to such notions.[4] Yet Cromwell manifestly stands at the centre of whatever was being planned and done. Thus, before the reformist labours of the 1530's can be properly assessed, we must come to some positive conclusions about Cromwell's own personality and intentions.

It is certainly true that the Cromwell usually found in the books would hardly be seen as a man of ideas and ideals. He may no longer be thought of as a mere executive agent, the willing and useful servant of his master's autocratic determination, but that is not to endow him with positive plans for reform and renewal. An energetic administrator who gave English government a new cast, perhaps; a scrupulous executor of severe policies; even perhaps a man sympathetic to some of the new ideas in religion which were spreading through the realm in his days of

---

[1] Zeeveld, *Foundations*, 113.
[2] Ferguson, *Articulate Citizen*, 134.
[3] McConica, *English Humanists*, 191.
[4] Jones, *Tudor Commonwealth*, 31.

power;[5] but does any of this support a view which would turn him from an employer of writers useful to the political changes into the leader of a movement for comprehensive reform? I have before this suggested that his mind inclined to intellectual speculation, and that his relations with Thomas Starkey's work display him as an active participant in a dialogue between thought and action,[6] but I agree that I have not yet succeeded in describing a Thomas Cromwell who would really fit that role.

Yet to do so is not really very difficult.[7] The inadequacy of the conventional picture emerges in odd ways. Cromwell, we know, had no formal schooling, and we therefore assume, with the usual arrogance of educators, that however bright a mind he may have possessed he cannot have been attuned to the theorizing and formal planning beloved by intellectuals. Yet this uneducated man received letters in Latin, with Greek bits in them, and not only from tufthunters but also from a man like Richard Morison who knew him well and meant his letters to be read. He spoke and read Italian and French with obvious fluency. Most surprising of all, he was something of an artist in English. On the basis of his surviving letters it has been concluded that his style displayed an 'extraordinary liveliness and flexibility of usage', marked by the employment of a 'large number of loan words, new formations and words modified in meaning',[8] and this opinion would draw only support from a study of the state papers and statutes he drafted. A man whose mind operated in such an inventive use of language has at least the makings of an intellectual.

The best start for a proper appreciation of Cromwell's intellect

[5] Cf. my *Tudor Revolution in Government* (Cambridge, 1953) and *Policy and Police* (Cambridge, 1972); A. G. Dickens, *Thomas Cromwell and the English Reformation* (London, 1959).

[6] G. R. Elton, 'The Political Creed of Thomas Cromwell,' *Trans. Royal Hist. Soc.* (1956), 69ff.; 'Reform by Statute,' *Proc. Brit. Acad.* liv (1968), 165ff.

[7] A. J. Slavin, in his introduction to his selection of Cromwell's letters (*Thomas Cromwell on Church and Commonwealth*, Harper Torchbooks, 1969), has painted a generous picture of a passionate and universal reformer. Though overdone, and too much based on McConica's misleading analysis, it seems to me essentially correct.

[8] Audrey le Lièvre, 'Linguistic Activity among Statesmen at the Court of Henry VIII, with reference to contemporary letters, and especially those of Thomas Cromwell,' unpublished dissertation (Cambridge, 1949); quotation at p. 168.

is the earliest interpretation offered by a university man. Gabriel
Harvey, the Elizabethan critic and scholar, reflecting in the
margins of his books on topics of statecraft, careers in office, and
the use of power, found Cromwell especially interesting and
impressive.[9] He recognized, of course, that there was an absence
of formal training and learning, but did not conclude from this
that Cromwell lacked intellectual attainments. The late minister
merited Harvey's highest term of praise, 'a Roman disposition':

All the stringes of your Tongue & powers of your speech euer
loosed & present. The instruments & powers of your wit &
speech, euer most reddy with facility. All the L. Cromwells
commendation, sauing a natural heroical audacity and sum
pragmatical experience. . .The Lord Cromwell, of A Romane
disposition, in his kynd a Marius or Sylla. Smal Lerning, but
nobely minded & Industrious, with sufficiency of common
witt, vtterance, & experience.[10]

The best career in office, thought Harvey, was that built by the
man himself, without the advantages of birth or royal favour:
'Vt olim Marius, sed praecipue Caesar: ut nuper apud nos
Cromuellus.'[11] Cromwell was certainly being elevated to distinguished company, though another set of comparisons might have
pleased him less. To Harvey, a Roman disposition involved also
a spirit of adventure, 'plus Virtutis quam Artis', which among
Englishmen he discovered in an oddly assorted foursome: Cromwell, Northumberland, Thomas Stukeley and Francis Drake.[12]
But in the main he saw in Cromwell high natural abilities put to
excellent use: 'A cleare light of witt, with A divine method, &
singular dexterity jn al his sayings & doings.'[13] He recognized the
superiority of experienced skill over book-learning: Cecil's political dexterity put Thomas Smith's intellectualism in the shade,
and Cromwell's far-flung practical energy overcame Gardiner's
massively trained prudence.[14] This sounds like the conventional

---

[9] *Gabriel Harvey's Marginalia*, ed. G. C. Moore-Smith (Stratford on Avon,
1913). In quoting I have extended abbreviations and slightly modified
punctuation. One note, not relevant here, offers support to a point I tried
to make in my *Tudor Revolution*: 'Mr Cromwell, afterward Lord Cromwell, augmentid the commodity and authority of euerie office that he
attainid' (p. 196).

[10] Ibid. 193, 196.   [11] Ibid. 196.   [12] Ibid. 141.   [13] Ibid. 156.

[14] Ibid. 149: 'Smithaeis Literulis praeluxit Caecilianus πολιτισμος, et poly-

juxtaposition of the successful man of action and the failed man
of letters, but Harvey knew better: 'The L. Cromwell, by the only
promptness of his wit, facility of speech, & A pragmatical dexterity to all purposes, ouershadowed and obscured euen our
greatest clarkes.'[15]

This is an interesting opinion, the more so because Harvey
seems to have had information on Cromwell as a speaker and
orator of which we are otherwise ignorant. All great men
('Megalandri'), he thought, were outstanding orators either by
nature or by art, and Henry VIII had found four such 'heroici
Consiliarij': 'Cardinalis Volsaeus, Prorex Cromuellus, Cancellarius
Morus, pragmaticus Gardinerus'.[16] 'Prorex', not perhaps 'Secre-
tarius': this well-read man, born a few years after Cromwell's
death, seems to have had a very proper understanding of the
great man's real position in the realm. That is by the way; what
matters is whether those favourable opinions, possibly based on
things we no longer know about, can be supported by evidence
still extant. What proof is there that Cromwell's natural intelligence and energy also showed themselves in activities which
could fairly be described as overshadowing and obscuring 'even
our greatest clerks'?

We possess two catalogues of Cromwell's papers and archives
which throw some light on his interests. Both were compiled
early in his official career, which in the circumstances is helpful
in that they therefore display his collection before he became the
recipient of everybody's bright ideas and before the needs of the
realm he administered dictated the kind of thing he acquired and
kept.[17] The main part of those long lists consists of what might
have been expected: bills to be promoted with the King, warrants,
a good deal of parliamentary material which must engage us
later, private matters – Cromwell's business archive. But among
them are less routine materials. The numerous papers concerned

---

pragmatica Cromelli Industria polytechnicam Gardineri prudentiam
superauit.'
[15] Ibid. 91.   [16] Ibid. 122.
[17] The catalogues are E 36/143, fos. 1–22, and E 36/139, fos. 42–88,
calendared in *LP* vi. 299 and vii. 923. The first is described as listing
papers collected since November 1532; the second as those acquired
between Michaelmas 1531 and Michaelmas 1533. There are not enough
overlaps to make those dates altogether convincing, and some later stuff
seems certainly to have been added. Nevertheless, the bulk of the archive
belongs to 1532–3.

with the Divorce, the power of the pope and the rights of the Crown need not surprise us, though attention is arrested as one comes across proof of Cromwell's own activity (a minute drawn by him 'concerning the King's great cause') or of wider interests in the papacy than mere involvement in the politics of the day might explain ('an oration for Pope Julius XII [sic]', 'a book reciting what is the perverse Church'). But there are a good many less obvious things. Some evince a general curiosity: a book bound in parchment called 'Of Desire in Forma Iuvenis', a set of Italian verses, a short interlude or prologue 'Of Pleasure and Disport', an argument between the Archangel Raphael and some gentlemen of England, 'an old bill how Abraham taught the seven sciences', a dialogue between Pasquillius and Maforius, a book on the society and clergy of Venice, a collection of speeches made by the prophets of the Old Testament in addressing kings. There is an interest in politics: a copy of the advice tendered by King Louis of France to his son Philip, an illustrated book ('made with figures') about the King's 'power royal'. The law makes its appearance in more than merely practical ways: a paper about the training of notaries, a copy of Charles V's message to the supreme court of the empire (translated into English), and a philosophic essay on the theme that 'where laws is not right used, justice is abused'. 'A book in paper made in French much necessary for the Parliament' may well have been a copy of the *Modus Tenendi Parliamentum*. History, too, was among the interests of a man who possessed a brief chronicle of England, another 'of Brute coming into this realm', a 'book of Concilium Bonifacii apud Westmonasterium', and an account of the trial of two bishops in Henry II's reign for proclaiming the papal interdict. The fact that these materials may in part be said to refer to Cromwell's political tasks signifies nothing: I am trying to show that in tackling those tasks he employed the mind of a reader and student, not that he was spending his time in learned relaxation.

The largest collection of such non-routine papers relates to the problems of the English economy. This may not be surprising, but the range and variety – even leaving out the draft bills of Parliament – are impressive. Problems of the textile industry predominate: a book about the Staplers of Calais, a parchment roll giving the price of wool and profit of wool sales in Calais and

London respectively, another statistical record concerning cloth
shipped to Antwerp by merchant strangers, devices touching the
damaging import of silken goods and the manufacture of broad-
cloth and kersies. There is a paper about this last matter from
Cromwell's own pen. An 'advice' for improving the system of
taxation runs well with two papers about deficiencies in the
customs service, so detrimental to the royal finances. But some
items show a more positive interest in reform, as 'the remembrance for sorting the inclosures', the memorandum on the
causes of impoverishment in South Wales, or the two sets of
articles 'for a commonwealth', one by Cromwell's old friend
Stephen Vaughan and one anonymous. There is even a somewhat
mysterious proposal 'for reformation of a common wealth within
the Castle of Dover'. But perhaps the most revealing pieces are
those which present statistically useful information: a record of
parish churches in the realm, a register of creeks and havens, a
tally of Yorkshire clothmakers. They indicate the kind of mind
which was to organize the *Valor Ecclesiasticus* and set up parish
registers. Especially when we remember that what those catalogues list are working papers, not a gentleman's library (and we
only know that Cromwell possessed books, not what they were)
it becomes apparent that his concern with principle and research
makes it very inadequate to see in him nothing but a pragmatic
exploiter of other people's ideas.

Thomas Cromwell was no philistine; trained or not, he cared
about the concerns of the mind. Among his close friends he
counted Sir Thomas Elyot, the most prolific popularizer of ideas
of the day,[18] and Sir Thomas Wyatt, England's finest poet.[19]
Neither of these wrote propaganda for the government or even
published the sort of 'advanced' book which has been classified
as embodying Cromwell's 'Erasmianism'; his relations with these
men sprang from personality, not politics. Clever and learned
though they were, they do not perhaps qualify for Harvey's
phrase about 'our greatest clerks', but with men of that stamp
Cromwell also showed up well. He out-argued, rather than over-
bore, Sir Thomas More in the discussion in which he greatly

[18] Elyot and Cromwell had been well acquainted since about 1519, and
even serious political disagreements did not part them in the 1530's
(Lehmberg, *Elyot*, 32–3, 166–7).
[19] Wyatt recorded their relationship in the poem beginning 'The pillar
perished is whereto I leant . . .'.

embarrassed the ex-chancellor by reminding him of his own persecuting activities in his days of power,[20] and he had very much the better of an exchange with Fisher whom he convicted of using a double standard in judging what might be the law of God.[21] Of course, Cromwell was bound to concern himself with the practical uses of learning, but that was never the whole of it, as his interest in history – already plain from his collection of chronicles – testifies. He was always on the alert for historical writings. In 1533, anxious to know more about the background to the Lutheran Reformation, he had his German expert Christopher Mont start on a translation of German chronicles and asked Stephen Vaughan to obtain him half a dozen such books which he understood had lately been translated into Latin.[22] In 1535, the prior of Christchurch (Hants.) sent him, as requested, a copy of 'Beda *de ecclesiastica historia* and another chronicle whose author I do not know; wherein is also another treatise whose title is *de gestis pontificum Anglorum'*. The prior regretted that another book asked for by Cromwell, 'De Gestis Anglorum', had not been traced; it would be sent as soon as found.[23]

This interest in the past had its practical side; after all, Cromwell based the first of his revolutionary statutes, the 1533 Act of Appeals, on the testimony of 'divers and sundry histories and chronicles'. But how much genuine antiquarian interest was mingled with the desire to find useful precedents in the past for present practices is neatly illustrated in a letter from Thomas Bedyll (a close acquaintance) who in July 1536 was going through the muniments of Ramsey Abbey.[24]

> I found a charter of King Edgar written in a very antique
> Roman hand, hard to read at the first sight and light enough
> after that a man found out six or seven words and after com-
> pared letter to letter. I am sure ye would delight to see the
> same for the strangeness and antiquity thereof. In the end
> thereof is subscribed thus: Signum Ædgari incliti et
> serenissimi anglorum imperatoris. Whereby it may well be
> noted that afore the Conquest the said king wrote himself to

[20] *The Correspondence of Sir Thomas More*, ed. Elizabeth F. Rogers (Princeton, 1947), 557–8.

[21] Merriman, i. 373–9.   [22] *LP* vi. 717, 1448.

[23] SP 1/97, fo. 112 (*LP* ix. 529).   [24] BM, Cleo. E. iv, fo. 233 (*LP* x. 90).

be emperor of England. Item, it is to be noted of the sub-
scription of the said charter that in England were six dukes at
the time. For they subscribed this: Ego Alfwold dux. Ego
Athelstan dux. Ego Ælfre dux. Ego Oslac dux. And that time
the king had two sons, Edward and Athelred, which he subscribed not at dux but under this manner: Signum Ædwardi
eiusdem regis filii – Signum Æthelredi fratris eius.

I have seen also there a charter of King Edward written
afore the Conquest, which beginneth thus: in onomate supremi
kuriou, and soon afore the same he writeth thus: Ego
Ædwardus totius Albionis dei moderante gubernatione
[blank] Archiepiscopis, Episcopis [etc.]. . .whereby ye may
note that King Edward nameth himself [blank] of all Albion
and not by the name of England. . .King Edward by his kingly
power could exempt this monastery of Ramsey from all
bishops' powers. The King's grace may as well exempt all
other abbeys or as many as he will from the bishops' powers.
And to this charter subscribed four dukes – Leouricus,
Haroldus, Leofwynus and Eadwynus.

Bedyll, whose palaeographical skill seems to have let him down
at a crucial point, naturally drew attention to the usefulness of
this ancient precedent for the King's imperial control of the
Church, but he understood Cromwell well enough to add the
kind of detail that would be of interest only to an enthusiast.
Another of Cromwell's good friends was the leading historian of
the day, Edward Hall, who in 1533, writing for a present of
venison from the King's stock on the occasion of the dinner he
was to give as reader at Gray's Inn, signed himself 'tuus totus et
si quid toto plus esse possit' and in a postscript added that he
was forwarding a map of Hungary and a portrait of Andrea
Doria lately received from Cologne.[25]
That Cromwell was profoundly interested in writers and
writings is well known now, as it was well known at the time.
Though it is not possible to go all the way with McConica who
sees Cromwell officially promoting every piece of reformist
literature from about 1532 or 1534 onwards, it is also not necessary to suppose with him that the undoubted activity there was

[25] SP 1/77, fo. 126 (*LP* vi. 741): 'Mitto tibi Cartam Vngarie et Imaginem
Andree Dorie heri ex Colonia missas.'

reflects only a concern to overcome the vigorous conservative production of the early 1530's and to publish propaganda.[26] One who knew all about Cromwell's interests was Henry, Lord Morley who in 1539 sent him a copy of Machiavelli's *History of Florence* and referred to the *Prince* in terms which have become famous but remain far from clear.[27] George Spalatin, from Wittenberg, sent a more conventional treatise on 'the Solace and Consolation of Princes' by the hands of the astronomer Nicholas Crantzer which Cromwell in February 1539 forwarded to Henry who may have needed it more (and who was its intended destination).[28]

[26] McConica, *English Humanists*, ch. 5 (see his summing-up on pp. 147–9). His account is marred by a number of factual errors. Erasmus, who died in 1536, is said to have been unable to recall something eighteen years after 1529 (p. 107). The *praemunire* attack of 1531 did not take place in Parliament (p. 109). The words 'supreme head' were added to the King's style in 1535, not 1531 (p. 111). No one took a stand against the 1532 Supplication in the Lords where the matter never came up (p. 126). The Thomas Berthelet who offered his services in 1533 was not the King's printer but an ex-secretary of Wolsey's (p. 136). The translating on which Sadler was engaged in 1533 touched despatches, not literature (p. 143). It is more important that the picture of Cromwell's general gathering in of writers depends in part on unacknowledged speculation. The long list, on p. 127, of 'King's recruits' mostly collected by Cromwell includes some (Morison, Starkey, Taverner) properly so described; some (Sampson, Fox) who held Crown appointments for years before they wrote in favour of the Divorce and did not owe either their office or their literary employment to Cromwell; some (like Vaughan and Rastell) who, though linked with Cromwell, never produced any serious writing; and at least one (Wakefield) whom McConica shows to have risen under quite different patronage. The connection between Cromwell's circle and Swinnerton is slender but convincing; that with Leonard Cox more tenuous but still just possible; but for Thomas Paynell even McConica can produce no connection at all. In any case, all these people had written the things that got them into McConica's list before they attracted official attention. The picture of a large body of men 'recruited' by Cromwell and working under official instruction is seriously misleading, a point which shall be more fully explained in ch. 3.

[27] SP 1/143, fo. 74 (*LP* xiv. I. 285). Morley described the *History of Florence* in such a way as clearly to identify it as Machiavelli's work, but he did not name the author. He went on: 'And furthermore, this book of Machiavelli *de principe* is surely a very special good thing for your lordship, which are so nigh about our sovereign lord in Council, to look upon for many causes, as I suppose yourself shall judge when ye have seen the same.' This suggests that the *Prince* was sent at the same time and that Morley did not think Cromwell already acquainted with it. But why mention Machiavelli as the author of only the second work? Did Morley not know who had written that history? If so, what put the *Prince* in his mind?

[28] Merriman, ii. 178.

More important in the present context, all sorts of men seeking favour or recognition bombarded Cromwell with their offerings. There is quite a list of these, but so mixed as to preclude any notion of deliberate solicitation. Florence Volusenus, the Scottish humanist, in 1531 presented a 'treaty of Historie', a poor thing which he hoped would do until he had something better to send. He trusted the King's new councillor would help to make peace between England and Scotland.[29] Martin Tyndale, fellow of King's College, Cambridge, and sometimes regarded as a younger brother of the great William, in 1533 offered a translation of Erasmus' lives of John Colet and John Vitruvius, discovered 'in a great book called Erasmus' Epistles, where a man would have little thought to have found them'. He hoped to make Colet, half forgotten in England, to 'walk about in his country' again where he had engendered so much spiritual progeny.[30] Tyndale, who had some pertinent things to say about the difficulty of translating,[31] needed a patron to enable him to continue his studies: his parents, who had first supported him, had fallen on evil days, while Dr Denton, dean of Lichfield, who had come to the rescue with an exhibition, had recently died. Since Martin continued in his studies and his fellowship till about 1539,[32] Cromwell may have helped him; but though he was acquainted with both Richard Taverner and William Marshall, certainly Cromwell's clients by this time, he did not himself enter

---

[29] SP 1/237, fo. 17 (*LP Add.* 731).

[30] SP 1/77, fos. 148–9; BM, Harl. 6989, fo. 145 (*LP* vi. 751–2). Cf. McConica, *English Humanists*, 119–20. Tyndale referred to Cromwell's kindness to his brother John 'in his troubles'. John Tyndale, merchant of London, was in trouble late in 1530 for spreading the *Practice of Prelates*, and on the strength of some papers of John Foxe's he is thought to have been William's brother. William certainly had a brother John (John Foxe, *Acts and Monuments*, ed. Cattley, v. 803–4; *Calendar of State Papers Venetian*, iv. 271; J. F. Mozley, *William Tyndale* [London, 1937], 4, 21, 121–2, 170–2). But according to J. Venn, *Alumni Cantabrigienses*, Martin came from Surrey, not Gloucester. Since it is highly improbable that two John Tyndales got into trouble about 1530, Foxe's identification may well be wrong; certainly Martin (whose brother John was dead by 1533) claimed no relationship with William.

[31] 'It is not so easy to indict good English in translating as when one writeth his own inventions and cogitations.' He pointed out how new the practice was: before he started, the only translation he had seen had been Thomas Elyot's *Plutarch*.

[32] Venn, *Alumni Cant.*

service.[33] In 1535, the prior of Kingswood, Thomas Redinge, sought to win favour by submitting a short treatise on the royal supremacy, dedicated to Cromwell, but even so convenient and flattering a work never saw the light of print, and Redinge simply remained prior of his house till its dissolution on 1 February 1538.[34]

More relevant still is the position of John Robyns, a canon of Wolsey's (and the King's) College at Oxford, who kept supplying Cromwell with learned books, sent under covering notes written in Latin. On 19 December 1532, the two of them had a conversation during which Robyns promised a treatise on the price of corn – 'opusculum de vilitate et caristia annone' – and a work on the possessions of the Church. By March 1533 he had to admit that the first book had not got started (he now promised it for Easter with an additional essay on emeralds), while of the second only the first part, setting out the reasons why ecclesiastical wealth should be confiscated, was written; he would send it when the second part – 'que has rationes dissolvit' – was done. Robyns was a persistent non-finisher. In 1536 he regretted that illness had prevented him from presenting yet another promised book *de accidentibus futuris*, though he had managed to supply another work (seemingly not by himself) which explained what the stars foretold for England that year. He was not going to trouble Cromwell with the treatise on the price of corn (still unfinished) or another on the exchanges because he could see that nothing much was going to happen in these respects in 1536, certainly nothing to compare with the outstanding events of that year in which Cromwell would be busy enough. He concluded with a specious excuse that rings painfully familiar to any editor or publisher waiting for copy: he dared not write at greater length 'ne te gravioribus (ut semper) intentum negotiis disturbaram'.[35] Probably Cromwell was wise not to add this author to his stable, but Robyns and he were well acquainted, and the correspondence provides useful evidence of the sort of topics that interested the minister. Not that we have any other indication of an addiction to astrology.

[33] He became master of the school at St Albans; the date of his death is unknown (Thomas Harwood, *Alumni Etonienses* [1797], 144).
[34] *LP* viii. 79; xiii. I. 199.
[35] SP 1/75, fos. 48v, 71; 101, fo. 114 (*LP* vi. 262, 295; x. 121).

A more obvious purpose was intended by Peter Beckwith of Calais who in 1536 produced some fifteen pages of verses, in various classical metres, all in praise of Cromwell, the hammer of the pope, 'post regem prolemque suam non maior in oris'. Beckwith certainly thought that the minister and not the King had done the great deed: 'Episcopus Romanus per dominum Thomam Cromwell mediante regio auxilio sibi prestito ab Anglia expulsus est.' There is no sign that he got the hoped-for benefice or other reward.[36] In the same year, one William Cutler attended for a fortnight at Cromwell's house in hopes of presenting a book he had written 'for the instruction of ignorant people'; he had been encouraged by the countess of Oxford, but in the end had to leave the work with Cromwell's secretary.[37] Thomas Swinnerton, unconvincingly suspected by McConica of having an earlier contact with Cromwell, dedicated to him a long and tedious exposition of the interpretative techniques to be used in expounding Scripture, with a prefatory note which argues no measure of acquaintance.[38] Perhaps the oddest production to reach Cromwell came from Thomas Gibson, a printer and pamphleteer acquainted with Latimer but not previously known to Cromwell. He had compiled a tally of prophecies to prove that Henry VIII was the king chosen by God 'to win the holy cross and also divers realms'.[39] As his covering letter explained, 'the rude sort' were in error when they doubted that a king with so small a nation would be able 'to overcome so many realms': God, 'with a mighty stretched-out arm', would 'deliver his elect and deliver into our King's hands his enemies, yea, and will be his defence even as he was Gideon's who put to flight with 300 persons a mighty host who were in number as the sands on the sea bank'. Though he

---

[36] SP 1/102, fos. 80–7 (*LP* x. 356). Beckwith, writing to London, sent his verses to a friend from St Omer, but that they did reach Cromwell is confirmed by his clerk's docket.

[37] SP 1/113, fo. 176 (*LP* xi. 1459).

[38] E 36/192 (*LP* xi. 1422): 'The Tropes and Figures of Scripture'. He meant to debate when Scripture should be interpreted literally and when not, following St Augustine. Though favourably inclined to the new learning and convinced that works justify on earth only, he regretted the levity of the radicals who accepted a literal interpretation when it suited them and said 'the letter killeth' when it did not.

[39] BM, Cleo. E. vi, fos. 401–6 (*LP* xiii. II. 1242). The date is purely conjectural, and there is no reason to think that this piece was written later than early 1537 when Latimer mentioned Gibson's name to Cromwell. For Gibson see also below, p. 63.

disclaimed the learning and understanding required for a proper interpretation of prophecies, he had managed to gather thirteen from highly diverse sources, all fairly mad. Some common sense reasserted itself in a final note to the effect that prophecies touching the holy cross were not to be taken literally: they implied victory over 'the devil's minister, the bishop of Rome', and the restoration of the gospel. The general quality of Gibson's exalted compilation may be judged from the first item: St Thomas calls him who shall win the holy cross 'the king of virgins', and 'surely it seemeth very well to be our sovereign lord the King that now is' since he has chosen the true religion. Cromwell was no doubt well advised to ignore Latimer's half-hearted recommendation and give the printing of the *Bishops' Book* to the King's printer.

Still, these curious gifts indicate what it was believed would attract Cromwell's interest, and even when they had nothing tangible to offer a good many students and intellectuals sought favour by pushing their potential wares. Richard Guercius and Thomas Mynternus (Gwercy and Mintern?) laboured over long and flowery Latin panegyrics, with Greek bits in them to liven things up.[40] As Richard Morison put it, in the extravagant style much favoured in such communications: he well knew that there was hardly a man in England 'qui non modis omnibus cupiet, se dignitatis tuae studiosum declarare, ornatissime Crumwelle'.[41] Thomas Coventry, a monk of Evesham seconded to Oxford, in 1539 expressed a fairly common sentiment:

> The singular favour that your lordship beareth to the un-cloaked and pure teaching of the holy letters and Scripture of God causeth me to have an undoubted trust that your goodness will extend even to all such as reserve their endeavour, study and labour to the said your most godly purpose. Great pains in Hebrew, Greek and Latin I have taken, and that, I trust, not without profit, as mine especial friend and good master, Master Morison, knoweth and can inform your lordship, if it so be your pleasure.

He was now ready to use his learning in service against those 'which have painted a papistical and sophistical divinity and mixed the clear vein of God with man's dreams and fantasies'.

---

[40] BM, Tit. B. i, fos. 359–60; SP 1/104, fo. 118 (*LP* viii. 267; x. 1065).
[41] BM, Vitellius B. xiv, fos. 131–2.

However, the forthcoming dissolution of his house would leave him destitute; would Cromwell instruct the commissioners 'to assign to me a pension sufficient for the continuance of my study'? He got a pension of £10 a year, not over-lavish but quite good enough for what he said he wanted.[42] Another who earlier had used similar arguments was John Horwood alias Placett ('secundum papisticos'), a monk of Winchcombe, who in the latter half of 1535 bombarded Cromwell with appeals. He wished to be employed in writing against purgatory and other popish notions, and he offered a little treatise of his own to back up his plea that he might serve the good cause of proclaiming the royal supremacy. Finally he got an interview with Cromwell who told him to study some more, advice he followed by reading 'many old books and ragged pamphilions', and he was bringing along not only his own written conclusions but also some dangerous popish pamphlets and 'a book of physic' for Queen Anne. He even offered Cromwell money, though admittedly only a debt of £10 13s 4d allegedly owed to him by his abbot. Twice he besought Cromwell *in visceribus Christi*: once, for 'gracious counsel for the quietness of the inner man', the other time 'to save my honesty and to pay my debts and to buy me some books, to lend me 40s and to set me where I may have meat and drink'. But he never made it into employment.[43] The dissolution found him still at Winchcombe, and his pension of £6 will not have done much to quieten his inner man.[44]

In general, Cromwell showed both patience and kindness to such suitors. He took trouble with Horwood when he instructed him as to his studies, though the results do not seem to have encouraged further contact; he made William Swerder's day in 1536 when he publicly told him of the good things he was planning for him and his friends. 'Sunt enim, ut uulgo dici solet, πάντα τῶν φιλῶν κοινὰ.' Swerder, a client of Cranmer's, studied in Paris with Cromwell's encouragement and there was occasionally useful as a gatherer of intelligence. He maintained his tenuous contact with the minister and in 1539 sent him yet another 'little book' which he thought might please 'because it entreateth of

---

[42] SP 1/154, fo. 99 (*LP* xiv. II. 437); *LP* xv. 118.

[43] *LP* ix. 135; SP 1/96, fo. 127; 98, fo. 174 (*LP* ix. 321, 723).

[44] *LP* xiv. II. 728. The list contains no John Horwood but a William of that name. Since William appears nowhere else in the correspondence of those years, this may safely be guessed to be a mistake.

common wealths and diverse matters thereunto pertaining'.[45]
More importunate than most was Richard Richardin, a Scotsman
who in April 1536 hoped to secure entry into the secretary's
service by an original plea: 'Your lordship hath of all nations in
your service except Scottish, which I think were as necessary for
diverse causes and service as any other. For where they are true
and kind they will die for their master and lord. . .'. He summed
up the attitude of all these seekers after advancement when he
said he knew that in Cromwell's company he would get 'lordly
reward' and 'great wisdom'. But he made the mistake of over-
doing things: by pressing his suit 'in the time of your lordship's
great business of Parliament' he caused offence which he tried to
wipe out by some intensive crawling in partly incomprehensible
Scots. Still, he received some encouragement – a licence to preach
and at last a living. True to his habit he at once sought favour
again: could he have the burden of his first fruits reduced?[46]

The besieging of Thomas Cromwell by impecunious men of
learning demonstrates his reputation as a patron to such men,
and it must not be thought that he invariably despatched them
with no more than a courteous hearing and some small reward.
Apart from the familiar names among his scholar-clients, we
glimpse others, like that Master Thomas Tybald described in
1540 as 'belonging to my lord privy seal', a man who, knowing
Germany, France and Italy, was 'singular well learned and of my
said lord highly favoured'.[47] Such more worldly learning attracted
Cromwell's attention to Thomas Barnaby who worked for him
and for King Henry for years as an agent in France. Barnaby
later told the story to William Cecil.[48] Keeping his eyes open
while trading to Normandy, he came to the conclusion that by
taking Le Havre the English could strangle French trade and
bring that country to its knees.

> I showed the same to my Lord Cromwell, and he sent me
> thither upon the King's cost; and I drew a plack of it to him. . .
> My Lord Cromwell conferred the matter with me and my

[45] SP 1/101, fo. 232; 165, fo. 53 (*LP* x. 224; xiv. II. 605). Cf. *LP* xiii. II. 25;
xiv. II. 492; xv. 38.
[46] SP 1/103, fos. 181–2; 114, fo. 3 (*LP* x. 734; xii. I. 5: the second letter is
really earlier than the first, which is dated precisely); *LP* xii. II. 1138.
[47] SP 3/8, fo. 42 (*LP* xv. 217).
[48] BM, Lansdowne 2, fos. 187–91, 1 October 1552. I owe this reference to
Mr D. L. Potter.

Lord Fitzwilliam that was then lord admiral, better than three or four hours, perusing the placket, and said if he lived, and that war should happen, it should be remembered, for it was worth the hearing.

Scholars, too, made it into some sort of employment, though short of the intensive relationship developed by men like Taverner and Morison. McConica may well be right in thinking that Leonard Cox, the learned and prolific schoolmaster of Reading, worked specifically for Cromwell once proof of his learning had got him into the presence;[49] and there is reason to think that Thomas Derby, one of Cromwell's secretaries later promoted to the clerkship of the Privy Council, was a bit of a scholar.

There may even have been a measure of organization, to the extent that in his last years Cromwell detailed one of his secretaries for this kind of work. This was Anthony Bellasis, LL.D., a Yorkshireman – his elder brother sat on the Council of the North – who entered service in the autumn of 1536. The very first mention of him shows him dealing on his master's behalf with a cleric engaged in preparing a learned sermon.[50] Bellasis came to specialize in three ways. More particularly than other secretaries he took over the bulk of Cromwell's patronage business.[51] His legal training equipped him especially for tasks of arbitration, and on behalf of his chief he became active in mercantile and Requests business: on two occasions he conveyed Cromwell's instructions to the masters of requests.[52] And thirdly, he acted as particular intermediary with intellectuals seeking favour and employment. It was with him that Cutler left the treatise he had been unable to deliver to Cromwell in person, and it was with him that Jacobus Gislenus Thalassius dealt when he tried to promote himself into employment as a writer and informant based on Heidelberg.[53] In 1539 Bellasis accompanied Cromwell on a

[49] McConica, *English Humanists*, 140–1.
[50] *LP* xi. 594. For other positive evidence of Bellasis as a regular member of Cromwell's staff see *LP* xiii. I. 88; II. 175; xiv. II. 318.
[51] *LP* xi. 877, App. 13; xii. II. 885, 996, 1175; xii. I. 682, 785; xiv. II. 402, 447, 477, 482, 501 (in which Nicholas Wotton asks him to prevent the bestowal of a bishopric!), 543; xv. 371, 410, 603, 1029(63).
[52] *LP* xiii. I. 1047; xiv. I. 807, 1279; xiv. II. 452; xv. 1029 (65); Req 2/9/189, 12/36.
[53] Above, p. 20; *LP* xiii. I. 1014, 1514–15.

visit to Cambridge, a recruiting ground for useful wielders of learned pens.[54] The extant examples are few, but no other servant of Cromwell's is ever found intervening in such matters; even people who claimed acquaintance with the likes of Marshall or Morison always wrote direct to the lord privy seal. In Cromwell's last three years, Bellasis apparently became something like the patronage secretary on the minister's staff, with particular responsibility for men of learning.[55]

Bellasis's activities indicate that Cromwell came to see the need for bureaucratic organization even in his unsystematic relations with the people who could be useful as intellectuals in government service. There need be no question that throughout his career the minister was on the look-out for such men or that his clientage included people specifically retained for that purpose. The fortunes of Starkey and Morison, so well described by Zeeveld, are familiar proof. Starkey had been responsible for bringing in Morison, and for a time it looked as though between them they had persuaded Cromwell also to call in Edmund Harvel, long resident at Venice. In March 1535, Harvel responded with profuse thanks to the secretary's offer to place him in the King's service;[56] soon after he wrote to Starkey: 'What will you say if I come one day to the court to keep you company? I am by the loving favour of my great Master Cromwell counsel led to come into England.' He thought he would do so as soon as his business permitted, but that would take the best part of a year. A little later he explained to his friend that if he accepted his chief reason would be 'to see Mr Secretary delight so much of men virtuous as he by effect declared unto you'.[57] But Harvel, Englishman Italianate, in the end hesitated to leave Venice, and the approach came to nothing. On the other hand, Richard

---

[54] *LP* xiv. II. 410.

[55] Oddly enough, he did not get anything for himself, promotion reaching him, with suspicious promptitude, on Cromwell's fall. In late June 1540 he paid the very considerable sum of £1062 14s 2d for a grant of the lands of Newburgh priory (*LP* xv. 831[84]); two months later he succeeded to a Worcestershire living vacated by the execution of Thomas Garret (ibid. 1027[46]); and in December that year he became one of the first prebendaries of the new cathedral of Westminster (*LP* xvi. 333). He abandoned the public career he had started under Cromwell, but he certainly made a good thing out of the minister's fall.

[56] SP 1/91, fo. 86 (*LP* viii. 373).

[57] BM, Nero B. vii, fos. 107, 116, 122 (*LP* viii. 511, 535, 579).

Taverner was in Cromwell's formal employ from about 1532 and William Marshall from at least 1536.[58] Stephen Vaughan at Antwerp, and John Uvedale, clerk of the Council of the North, also belonged to this inner circle of men actively engaged upon programmes of reform.[59] Others as evidently did not, including two of the most prolific pamphleteers of the decade, Christopher St German and Clement Armstrong.[60] All the indications are that one must not simply link every writer, reformer or humanist with Cromwell: particular evidence of connection is required. Cromwell does seem deliberately to have encouraged the assembling of a group of advisers whose chief usefulness lay in their ability to write propaganda and develop plans of reform, but the group was never large – some six or eight men perhaps, by no means all of them formally his servants or *familia* because he was quick to put some where they wished to be, in the service of the King. A larger number of men drifted around the edges of this circle, seeking entry or just seeking favour; by their very existence and such favours as came their way they demonstrated that Cromwell's concern extended beyond the immediate services to religion and politics that might be obtained from trained scholarly minds.

The reality of the situation was more personal and purely intellectual, less exclusively political, than is commonly understood. What it was like to attend upon Cromwell in this mood is very well described in a long anonymous letter probably written by John Oliver, master in Chancery, a leading civilian and canonist of the day.[61] Its likely date is 1538,[62] and it was called forth by

---

[58] For Taverner see McConica, *English Humanists*, 117–18, and below, pp. 61–2; for Marshall, below, p. 62, and *Policy and Police*, 186. McConica, 136–7, is wrong about the relationship between Cromwell and Marshall.

[59] For Vaughan see below, p. 61; for Uvedale, an ardent promoter of the English Bible, see especially SP 1/160, fo. 12 (*LP* xv. 648).

[60] For St German see *Policy and Police*, 173–4, and below, pp. 74–5; for Armstrong, S. T. Bindoff, 'Clement Armstrong and his Treatises of the Commonweal,' *Economic History Review* ser. 1, xiv (1944), 64–73, and below, pp. 69–70.

[61] SP 1/141, fos. 126–7 (*LP* xiii. II. 1223). The letter is not signed, and the handsome hand, which may be a clerk's, has not been identified. However, the writer gives a number of details about himself. He was trained as a canon lawyer; he learned Greek from Robert Wakefield (for whom cf. McConica, *English Humanists*, 134); some time in the very early 1530's he became a King's chaplain; he sat on the commission which made 'the new laws' and wrote the preface to them; he composed a sermon which Cranmer had sent to Cromwell; he was familiarly acquainted with two of

the fact that at their last meeting Cromwell had expressed a doubt whether Oliver had 'deposed those papistical dregs wherein I had been studied'. The radicals of the 1530's always had some difficulty in believing that men trained in the 'popish' canon law could be sincere in their conversion to the royal supremacy, and Oliver hastened to assuage suspicions by explaining in detail how he had come to change his views. He had never forgotten the first time he met Cromwell, 'in your law parlour in your old house at the Austin Friars'. He had been summoned to explain himself 'concerning the Lady Dowager's matter' (the Divorce) and had succeeded in convincing Cromwell that his personal opinion was on the King's side: he had spoken for the Queen only 'as I was enforced by the old bishop of Canterbury [Warham] which was then alive'. Cromwell had then most kindly restored him to the King's favour 'and did indeed put me not only to be his grace's chaplain but also procured unto me all that living that I have'. This was probably about the middle of 1531.[63] Ever since then Oliver had worked hard at problems of the faith, reading the Bible in English (one wonders which translation he used), comparing 'the Vulgate, which they call St Jerome's translation', with that of Erasmus – in fact, he 'did interline Erasmus' translation through the whole Testament in the other translation with my own hand from the beginning to the ending: I have the book yet to testify'. And since 'the New Testament was not first written in Latin but in Greek', he learned that language too and studied the gospels in the original. Lately he had started a course on the Fathers, both Greek and Latin. Nor need Cromwell suppose that 'all these labours might be taken and the judgment never a whit amended': a number of things he had recently written would show how he had benefited. As a clincher, he referred Cromwell

Cromwell's servants, Nicholas Arnold and Edward Draycott. The commission on the canon law, whose product is lost, included Richard Gwent (dean of the Arches), Edward Carne, John Hughes and John Oliver (*LP* ix. 549). Oliver is described as King's chaplain by 22 June 1531 (*LP* v. 306) and fits the other points in the letter better than the rest. Though the identification must be tentative, it will here be used, for convenience sake, as though it were certain.

[62] Fixed by a reference to Robert Barnes's presence in Wales 'last summer'; Barnes reached Wales by late March 1538 (*LP* xiii. I. 634).

[63] Cromwell lived at the Austin Friars' from at least 1527 till he moved to Stepney in the summer of 1533. Warham died in August 1532. Oliver (see preceding note) was King's chaplain by June 1531; Cromwell was not a King's councillor till late in 1530 (*Tudor Revolution*, 88).

to Robert Barnes, that trusty Lutheran, who would tell 'what he hath heard and known of my doctrine and communication in Wales this last summer'. He would rather be 'noted for a thief than a papist', and he hoped that Cromwell might live to Nestor's age.

The point here is what it was that had started him on this energetic course of study. When Cromwell had first decided to accept his explanations, he had gone to some lengths to teach Oliver a right way of thinking: in those early days he had several times invited him 'to your lordship's honourable board, divers dinners and suppers, where indeed I did hear such communications which were the very cause of the beginning of my conversion'.

> For me thought it were a stony heart and a blockish wit that could carry nothing away of such colloquy as was at your honourable board, and that made me to note them well. And when I came home to meet them with my English Bible, I found always the conclusions which you maintained at your board to be consonant with the Holy Word of God. And then I thought good to confer the English with the Latin throughout the whole Testament, and so I did, and then was I meetly well-settled in my conscience.

It was Cromwell's table-talk that initiated Oliver into a reformed way of Bible study. As early as 1531 or 1532, therefore, Cromwell was thinking along reformed lines and lines of evangelical theology, and dinner-time in his household was an occasion for learned discourse. As it happens, Oliver carried away new ideas in religion, but that is not to say that other ideas were not also debated. If this is how Cromwell conducted himself in the relaxed setting of mealtimes, there is no need to labour any further the argument that he treated learning and matters intellectual with zest and respect, and that he himself contributed independently to the discussion on fundamental issues that went on around him. He invited Oliver to those occasions because he wanted to let the talk work on his mind. Thus Thomas Cromwell's household at times assumed the aspect of a learned *salon*, inferior to, no doubt, but not essentially different from the goings on in Thomas More's household in the 1520's.

A man who could suppose that learned debate would help to

convert an opponent was likely to believe in the virtues of education, and a man like Thomas Cromwell who had had no formal
education himself was likely to rate those virtues high. We know
that he did. David Clapham, who at one time tutored young
Gregory Cromwell, has recorded his knowledge that the lord
privy seal especially wanted to ensure a good education for all.
The children of the upper classes were to be brought up properly
'in good literature'; other children 'after their abilities, wits and
aptness, in sciences and crafts'. To this safely Erasmian sentiment
(that is, the obvious ideal of any thoughtful person of the day)
Cromwell characteristically added an insistence that all education
should include an earnest instruction to 'obedience to God, to
the King's highness, and to such rulers and laws as his majesty
shall ordain'; but there is no need to doubt the sincerity of his
belief that all good education would benefit the recipient 'to the
great advancement of the common weal'.[64] In his First Injunctions to the Clergy (1536) Cromwell went out of his way to
arrange for the promotion of higher education: all incumbents of
benefices were to provide exhibitions for students at the Universities and grammar schools, each man maintaining one scholar
for every £100 of his annual income.[65] This sum necessarily
limited the command to the wealthiest clergy, but even so it
would, if ever put into proper effect, have provided a steady
stream of recruits to learning and a supply of trained men. The
Injunctions also explained what was in Cromwell's mind: these
scholars were either to become assistants in their patron's cure,
thereby improving the standards of the spiritual welfare provided, or 'when need shall be' were to contribute to the common
weal in other ways 'with their counsel and wisdom'. Cromwell
could not have more plainly announced his conviction that the
public service should include a body of recruits from the Universities, to augment and continue the kind of advisory group that
had collected around him.

He naturally took his own part in the provision of places at
Oxford and Cambridge, though we have no idea how many
students he supported. The words of others make certain that
there were far more than evidence has survived for. Richard

[64] Cited by McConica, *English Humanists*, 191.
[65] *Documents Illustrative of English Church History*, ed. H. Gee and
W. J. Hardy (London, 1896), 274.

Marshall, a poor scholar, begged to be added to his exhibitioners – 'inter tuos me numeres stipendiarios'.[66] Another man in a similar position used English, pressing Cromwell 'for the love of God and in the way of charity to take me as your scholar'.[67] Richard Mill, an ex-monk of Winchester, begged for Cromwell's intercession with the prior: he wished to be one of the six scholars whom the house was by its statutes supposed to maintain at Oxford. Not unnaturally, the prior jibbed at giving the exhibition to a man who had left the order and was noisily hostile to 'superstitious practices', but Cromwell tried, probably without success.[68] Established scholars also appealed to him, like Walter Graver, schoolmaster at Croyland, who, though only twenty-four, could not bear the climate, asked for another appointment, and mentioned Kirton near Burton as vacant; or perhaps Stamford which was wholesome and usefully close to Cambridge.[69] One hopes that his emphatic description of schoolmastering got him the job: he spoke feelingly of the endless labours needed to instruct boys in good letters, and of the unmanageably encyclopaedic knowledge required of a teacher.[70] John Man, lately reader in Greek at New College, hoped for an exhibition from the King to finance five years' study in France and elsewhere on the continent; he was encouraged in his application by Cromwell's 'incredible zeal in promoting good letters and your immense benevolence to all students'.[71] This sort of thing could pall, and a particularly empty encomium on this patron of scholars was disparagingly endorsed 'Edmund Sheffield's scholastical letters'.[72] These expressions of confidence in Cromwell's bounty to scholars must have had some substance behind them, even though the only actual payments I can discover are two sums of £5 to

---

[66] SP 1/156, fos. 5–6 (*LP* xiv. II. 758).

[67] SP 1/93, fo. 25 (*LP* viii. 828).

[68] SP 1/100, fos. 84, 85–6 (*LP* ix. 1128–9). Mill seems to have been a little unbalanced. He used the royal plural with reference to himself, but also called Cromwell prince and your majesty.

[69] SP 1/100, fos. 60–1 (*LP* ix. 1107).

[70] 'Quotiens complector animo...quanta molis, quamque inexhausti laboris opus sit, pueritiam in bonas erudire literas, simulque quam vasta quam incomprehensa sit illa Encyclopaedia que in ludo magistro requiritur...'.

[71] SP 1/104, fo. 307 (*LP* x. 1269): 'Incredibilis tua in promovendis bonis literis diligentia et summa erga studiosos benevolentia...valde me animavit.'

[72] SP 1/134, fos. 253–4 (*LP* xiii. I. 1409).

Alexander Alesius[73] and a regular exhibition maintaining his nephew William Wellifed at Cambridge.[74] Maintaining students has its problems: Wellifed proved a somewhat unsatisfactory scholar, though he promised to amend.[75]

If the policy of financing learning was to pay off, the question of the education provided naturally became important. From Clapham's encomium we learn that Cromwell believed in the humanist ideal of 'good letters' for the ruling sort and a proper training in their skills for the working classes. In this he exactly echoed the sentiments of Thomas Starkey who may well have influenced his thinking on the subject.[76] His own son was brought up on Erasmus' *Colloquies*, which is small wonder since that was perhaps the most popular schoolbook of the time, and rather more surprisingly on Fabyan's *Chronicle*; though whether the choice reflected Cromwell's views or the tutor's is not certain.[77] But while not much can be made of this mention of Erasmus,[78] it is known that Cromwell had a high respect for the great scholar. He had an opportunity to prove it in 1535 when Erasmus was trying to get the arrears of his pension out of the living of Aldington in Kent. The incumbent was Richard Masters who had got into deep trouble over the affair of the Nun of Kent, but even after he was pardoned he tried to evade his obligations by pretending that the living remained confiscated (which was untrue) and that in any case his predecessor, not himself, had undertaken to pay the pension. Both Cranmer and Cromwell offered to help, and both also contributed substantially with gifts, ten marks from Cranmer, and twenty angels, a sizeable sum, from Cromwell who (Bedyll informed Erasmus) 'favours you exceptionally and everywhere shows himself to be an ardent friend of your name'. Although Erasmus wrote a suitable letter of thanks, he seems to have been quite surprised and expressed his astonishment to Erasmus Schets at Antwerp, who knew Cromwell. Schets replied:

---

[73] *LP* xiv. II. 782 (May and Dec. 1537).
[74] Ibid. (April and Nov. 1537; Dec. 1538; Jan. and Feb. 1539). That Wellifed was Cromwell's nephew is stated in *LP* xiii. II. 967(54).
[75] *LP* xi. 548–51. These undated letters probably belong into 1538, the year during which his exhibition was stopped.
[76] Thomas Starkey, *Dialogue between Reginald Pole and Thomas Lupset*, ed. K. M. Burton (London, 1948), 142.
[77] Ellis, iii. I. 343–5.
[78] McConica, *English Humanists*, 191, sees too much significance.

'Audio hunc esse bonum et sincerum, doctos amantem, tuique devotum.' No doubt Erasmus had heard differently from his friends in More's and Fisher's circles, but Schets was right: Cromwell loved learned men and proved it to their doyen in that substantial fashion which Erasmus throughout his life showed he appreciated.[79]

Cromwell's main practical effect upon education sprang from the attention he gave to the Universities. He hardly needed to be told by Thomas Legh how important those institutions were and in what need to be properly ordered, 'where either will be found all virtue and goodness, or else the fountain of all vice and mischief'.[80] He took care to secure a place of influence as soon as he could. The deaths of Lord Mountjoy and Bishop Fisher enabled him to acquire the high stewardship and chancellorship of Cambridge in 1535,[81] though at Oxford he had to be content with placing a colleague.[82] He was certainly responsible for reforming injunctions issued at both places; and at both they found great favour with the innovating party. The fellows of Magdalen College, Oxford, offered thanks for the orders encouraging the study of Greek and improving other disciplines, brushing aside as mere nonsense the pretence of the reactionaries that the injunctions might be against the College statutes and declaring the ordinance to be proof of Cromwell's 'no faint zeal to the furtherance of learning'.[83] From Cambridge Legh reported that

> the students do say that you have done more good there for
> the profit of study and advancement of learning than ever any
> chancellor did this heretofore. . .Many of the heads, which be
> for the most part addicted to sophistical learning, were not
> content with all that we have done and therefore may fortune
> to labour to have some relaxation thereof.[84]

The injunctions were certainly generally regarded as a very serious break with tradition, a point well made in Richard

[79] *Opus Epistolarum Desiderii Erasmi Roterodami*, ed. P. S. and H. M. Allen, xi. 232–3, 300, 321.
[80] *Three Chapters of Letters relating to the Suppression of Monasteries*, ed. T. Wright (Camden Society, 1843), 66.
[81] C. H. Cooper, *Annals of Cambridge*, i (Cambridge, 1842), 371.
[82] Sir William Fitzwilliam succeeded More as high steward.
[83] SP 1/96, fos. 118–19; 101, fo. 104 (*LP* ix. 312; x. 109).
[84] SP 1/98, fo. 110 (*LP* ix. 708).

Layton's famous report that he and his fellow commissioners had
'put Duns in Bocardo'.[85] They were the same at both Universities, each receiving one set of orders from Cromwell as vicar-
general and an additional set from the persons (Legh and
Layton) he commissioned to administer the changes for him.[86]
But like so much University reform they do not, on closer inspection, quite live up to the fierceness of their reputation, and
significantly McConica has not claimed them – the most positive
and extensive thing the Cromwellian reformers did for learning –
as proof of 'official Erasmianism'.

In part they dealt with the enforcement of the royal supremacy,
but that does not concern us now, except to note that the most
drastic reform, the abolition of the study of the canon law,
resulted from the political changes. Otherwise, there are three
essential principles. The more prosperous Colleges were ordered
to institute two daily public lectures, in Greek and Latin. Late-
medieval scholasticism from Duns Scotus onwards was proscribed
altogether in the arts course and to some extent in the teaching
of divinity. All students were to be free to study Scripture for
themselves. Legh's subsidiary injunctions mainly attended to
administrative matters (which, however, included putting all the
affairs of all the Colleges temporarily at Cromwell's discretion),
but also enjoined the University to set up a public lecture in
Greek or Hebrew, the first germ of the regius professorships.[87]
While it is, therefore, true that a good many abuses were reformed
in 1535 and privileges curtailed, as far as scholarship went Cromwell confined himself to some practical measures for the promotion of 'good letters', to eliminating the canon law, to shearing
off the extravagances of disputatious subtlety which had grown
upon the exposition of the faith, and to modernising the arts
course. All this was well in line with common humanist thinking
on the contents of higher education, but it fell well short of the
standard Erasmian demands as well as of such innovations as the
trilingual colleges at Louvain and Paris. True to his temper,
Cromwell proceeded with circumspection, while making quite
plain the direction in which his inclinations lay. As we now know,

---

[85] *Suppression Letters*, 71.
[86] Cooper, *Annals of Cambridge*, i. 375–6, sufficiently summarizes the
original Latin.
[87] Hugh Kearney, *Scholars and Gentlemen* (London, 1970), 21.

the reforms of 1535 did not substitute 'humanism' for 'scholasticism', and the latter soon recovered a kind of ascendancy,[88] but the measures which had been taken in the direction of more meaningful and better ordered study were never rescinded and did some good.

Education, as Cromwell rightly recognized, was a means to an end. What were his ends, his intellectually based purposes? What sort of things filled the discussions at his dinner table and elsewhere? Oliver's recollections show that Cromwell talked about the interpretation of Scripture, and in the circumstances – since he was trying to wean Oliver from papist notions – he may be presumed to have concentrated on the forms of Church government supposedly prescribed in Scripture. However, there are powerful signs that Cromwell's interest in the Bible was not so exclusively political and pragmatical. Foxe casually mentions that in his youth, while travelling to and from Rome, he learned the whole of the New Testament by heart, in Erasmus' Latin version.[89] This story, usually derided, may look rather more probable in the light of Oliver's admission that he always found Cromwell accurate in his citations from Scripture; moreover, though Cromwell's youthful travels long predated the appearance of Erasmus' New Testament, we now know that he made another visit in 1517–1518, a date which fits Foxe's story.[90] In fact, it is hard to doubt that Cromwell was a man of the gospel, a familiar figure of the age. As he told the prior of Kingswood: by him 'the Word of God, the gospel of Christ, is not only favoured but also perfected, set forth, maintained, increased and defended'.[91] The English Bible of 1539, commanded into all churches by his Injunctions of 1538, should after all be regarded as his monument.

But if Cromwell believed in the Bible, what was his religion? Evangelism of that sort covered a wide range of positive beliefs. In 1530 Cromwell told Wolsey that he wished Luther 'had never

[88] William T. Costello, *The Scholastic Curriculum at Early Seventeenth Century Cambridge* (Cambridge, Mass., 1958).
[89] Foxe, *Acts and Monuments*, v. 363.
[90] This was discovered by Mrs Dorothy Owen in the municipal accounts of Boston (Lincs.), the town on whose behalf Cromwell undertook the journey (thus confirming another of Foxe's tales: v. 363–4). I am most grateful to Mrs Owen for the information.
[91] SP 1/89, fo. 57 (*LP* viii. 79).

been born',[92] but nine years later he said to the envoys of the League of Schmalkalden, in confidence, that with respect to religion he was of their mind though, the world standing as it did, he would believe even as his master the King believed, and were he to die for it.[93] These Lutheran leanings do not look entirely convincing – diplomacy might so easily have played its part in that remark – and he has in consequence been claimed for that Erasmian freemasonry which recent historians have discovered in every part of Europe. Yet when Richard Taverner, assuredly a conscious disciple of Erasmus, received from Cromwell instructions to translate certain books, the works chosen were Lutheran – the Augsburg Confession, Sarcerius' *Commonplaces*, and Capito on the Psalms.[94] When the translator attended to the doctor of Rotterdam he succeeded in making him look like his counterpart from Wittenberg – a clear case of *Erasmum in Martinum*.[95] Up to a point, the distinction is unreal, a point neatly brought out in a treatise on the sacrament (1537) which invokes two guiding stars for a moderate, middle-of-the-road doctrine:

> Erasmus, a man worthy of fame, put forth a book wherein he showed the way how the discussion might be ended; Philip Melanchthon, desiring nothing more than peace, declared that the controversy of the number of sacraments was rather in words than in things.[96]

Lutheran philosophy, and especially the adiaphoristic doctrine associated with Melanchthon and Bucer, and in England with Starkey (and Cromwell), owed a good deal to Erasmus, but Erasmus, as we all know, was no Lutheran. In fact, Erasmus –

---

[92] Merriman, i. 327. [93] Ibid. 279.

[94] Taverner stated explicitly that the first and last of these works were translated at Cromwell's command; Sarcerius' book he chose himself but dedicated to Cromwell. He also told the King in 1539 that for three years Cromwell had commissioned various translations from him. See prefaces to STC 908, 21753, 23710 (CUL, Syn . 8 . 53 . 27; BM, 3128 . a . 33 and C . 53 . i . 25).

[95] Below, p. 75 n. 74.

[96] SP 6/2, fos. 130v–131. The date of this treatise (which extends over fos. 130–153v: LP Add. 1231) is given by the mention of the General Council called 'in Italy'. Since the King is still called only lord of Ireland, this must refer to the meeting at Mantua. – I know that some Erasmian enthusiasts wish to claim Melanchthon for their camp, but it would be absurd to overlook the fact that he was in the first place a Protestant.

not to put too fine a point on it – remained a papist to his dying
day. Cromwell, as we have seen, respected and admired Erasmus,
but to a man who so totally rejected the claims of the papacy the
philosopher offered no usable form of religion. The recent concentration on the many irenic and merely reformist touches in the
sixteenth-century debate on religion – particularly strong in the
1530's, the last decade of possible reunion – has too readily
ignored that fundamental problem: Erasmus, and the Erasmians
proper, did not break with Rome, England and Cromwell did, and
therefore Cromwell was speaking a cool truth when he said that
in general he inclined to the Protestant side. However, he was
neither frantic nor extremist. His speech to the Parliament of
1540 anticipated Henry VIII's more famous address of 1545 in
demanding the middle way, though it went one better by giving
to that middle way a positive virtue and by emphasizing the
supremacy of Scripture, evidently the core of Cromwell's religious
beliefs.[97] Thomas Cromwell was essentially an evangelical who
found things to use in humanist thought, not (like some of his
leading servants among the writers) a humanist who came to see
that circumstances compelled him reluctantly to opt for Protestantism. John Foxe really got him right – or a part of him.

However, Cromwell was also a minister of state, a King's
councillor with extensive duties and opportunities in the ordering
of the commonwealth. In these concerns, too, it is clear that he
worked from first principles and thought extensively; nothing
could be further from the truth than the notion that he simply
attended to such problems as came to notice. He had general
ideas and he planned ahead. His deep concern for the commonwealth was widely known and often referred to: three examples
will suffice. In 1534, Bishop Longland excused himself for not
raising a personal question before this 'for that I know your great
continual business for the common weal, which I am loath to
let'.[98] In 1535, Sir John Aleyn, alderman of London, pleaded 'for
the common wealth of all [the King's] subjects the which I know
well hath been ever your mind and intent to this day'.[99] And in
1536, John Barlow, dean of Westbury, offering to help stamp out
papists in the diocese of St David's, explained that he knew 'the
good zeal that your mastership beareth to the commonwealth, as

---

[97] *LJ* i. 128–9. For Henry's speech see Hall, *Chronicle*, 864–6.
[98] SP 1/83, fo. 168 (*LP* vii. 541).   [99] *StP* i. 443.

by the reformation of many things lately by your high policy and wisdom done to all men evidently doth appear'.[100] How fully we should see Cromwell himself in command of this commonwealth policy is something that still needs considering and shall be investigated in the next chapter, but those appreciations fairly assessed the purpose and effect of his administration. Cromwell was proud of that work: even at the very last when he was using every device to move Henry to a mercy which the fallen minister best knew had long since dried up he spoke without apology about his government of the realm:

> As to the commonwealth, I have after my wit, power and knowledge travailed therein, having had no respect to persons (your majesty only excepted and my duty to the same), but that I have done any injustice or wrong wilfully I trust God shall bear me witness and the world not able justly to accuse me.[101]

The man who urged a judge investigating a riot in which one of the lord privy seal's servants stood accused that he should proceed to a thorough search for the truth, without any favour, was entitled to that boast.[102]

[100] SP 1/101, fo. 13 (*LP* x. 19).
[101] Merriman, ii. 265.
[102] St Ch 2/21/243 (11 July [1537]), a letter from Cromwell to Sir Anthony Fitzherbert and Sir John Talbot who had a commission to examine a dispute between James Lawson and Cromwell's servant Thomas Lawson. 'Although', Cromwell wrote, 'I doubt not but ye will proceed therein as equity and justice shall require, yet I thought it expedient to desire you to take some pains therein, the rather for my sake, that the truth therein may thoroughly appear.' But appearances notwithstanding, he was not here seeking to exercise influence on his servant's behalf. For he went on to ask Fitzherbert also to look into an indictment for riot which had charged Thomas Lawson with breaking and entering: would he please interrogate the jury and report his findings so that 'I may cause such an order and direction therein as the case shall rightfully require.' The whole tenor of the letter makes it plain that Cromwell refused to assist his servant merely on the man's say-so and was anxious to act justly, irrespective of personal relationships.

3

CROMWELL AND HIS MEN

In order to see how Cromwell operated, what his reliance on
intellectuals amounted to, and how original he himself was, I
propose to consider his relations with members of the group, and
especially with the three of them about whom we know most –
Stephen Vaughan, Thomas Starkey and Richard Morison.

Stephen Vaughan and Thomas Cromwell were old friends.
Vaughan was a London merchant who entered Cromwell's service
probably in 1524 and remained in it even after his own affairs
took him to Antwerp in December 1527, as representative of the
Merchant Adventurers. Every time he returned to England he
busied himself on Cromwell's behalf: in 1528, for instance, he
looked after his master's London house while Cromwell was at
Oxford engaged on founding Wolsey's College there, and in
1529 he did likewise when Cromwell visited Ipswich in connection with the College there.[1] Throughout, however, their relations
were closer and more equal than this master–servant situation
might suggest, and some time in the 1530's Vaughan left Cromwell's service to enter the King's in which he remained to the end
of his life.[2] Their friendship was rarely troubled, although
Vaughan's enthusiastic temperament needed the curb which
Cromwell applied at times.[3] In doing so, Cromwell showed a
good deal of patience.

There is reason to think that Vaughan may have been responsible for introducing Cromwell to the virtues of Lutheranism. He
himself was first accused of heresy in August 1529, by the

[1] *LP* iv. 166, 2538(8), 3675, 4107, 5117, 5398.
[2] Vaughan was mentioned in Cromwell's will, dated 2 July 1529; at a later
date the word 'sometime' was inserted before the description of him as
'my servant' (*LP* iv. 5772). The main facts of Vaughan's public life are
collected in W. C. Richardson, *Stephen Vaughan, Financial Agent of
Henry VIII* (Baton Rouge, 1953).
[3] Ellis, ii. II. 215–16 (*LP* viii. 302), an undated letter addressed to Cromwell as secretary (1534–6), shows that he could be very angry with his
friend. But it all passed off.

Antwerp governor of the Adventurers: he claimed that the charge was malicious, supported only by the suborned testimony of a whore, and easily rebutted.[4] This may well have been so, but that Vaughan leant towards those dangerous opinions came out strongly in the well-known attempt he made to recruit Tyndale and Frith for the King's service. The story of those negotiations, begun in January 1531 and terminated abruptly in May when Henry put the kibosh on them, does not need retelling here, but some of the details are relevant and have been commonly mis-stated.[5] Both Demaus and Merriman assumed that the attempt was made on Cromwell's initiative and with Henry's knowledge; the former also supposed that what put an end to it was the King's reading of Tyndale Practice of Prelates, with its attack on the Divorce.[6] That the second point is wrong was recognized by Merriman: the book which so displeased Henry was Tyndale's reply to More, sent over by Vaughan who had made a fair copy of the author's manuscript.[7] But, as Tyndale himself knew, the Practice of Prelates had infuriated Henry in early 1530, and More had included it among the books prohibited by proclamation a full year before Vaughan approached Tyndale.[8] The King, who had been delighted by the reformer's earlier work on The Obedience of a Christian Man, had thereafter become quite sure that Tyndale was a detestable heretic, and it is totally improbable that in early 1531 he would have encouraged Vaughan's enter-prise. Neither, one supposes, would Cromwell if he had read the Practice.

So far as it goes, the evidence does indeed saddle Vaughan with the initiative. He returned to Antwerp in November 1530, after a short visit to England, but his first letters back say nothing about Tyndale and refer only to commercial and political matters discussed with Cromwell before leaving.[9] However, while in England, Vaughan had learned that Tyndale might return upon promise of a safe-conduct, information which he could not have got from Cromwell or the King but only from some closer

[4] LP iv. 5823.
[5] The best account is in R. Demaus, William Tyndale (London, 1886), ch. 10.
[6] Demaus, Tyndale, 271–2, 282; Merriman, i. 99–102.
[7] This is plain from Cromwell's letter of May 1531 (Merriman, i. 335–6).
[8] TRP i, no.122; for the date cf. Policy and Police, 218 n.5.
[9] LP iv. 6744, 6754; v. 26.

acquaintance of Tyndale's.[10] While it is a little improbable that
Cromwell should have had absolutely no inkling of what
Vaughan was going to do, it is clear that Henry had none; and
there is no sign that anyone in high places had authorized any
promises. Vaughan brought the matter into the open on 26 January
1531 when he wrote to Henry about his attempts to find Tyndale
and persuade him to return: he would promise the reformer to try
for the necessary safe-conduct, more likely to be granted now
when the political atmosphere had changed so much in England.[11]
The covering note to Cromwell – 'I pray you, let me know how
the King taketh my letters'[12] – shows clearly that this was to
be the first that Henry had heard of the business. He had indeed
shown an interest in the forthcoming book which Tyndale was
rumoured to be writing in reply to More, but that was a long way
from 'recruiting' Tyndale: the jump from one fact to the other
was one of Vaughan's characteristic rashnesses. However, Henry
did not immediately stop the negotiations; he decided to wait
until he had seen that book. It may be conjectured that he was
also trying out his new councillor, whose friend (for all Henry
knew, with his connivance) was so innocently taking up with a
notorious heretic and opponent of the Divorce. We know the
outcome: by May Henry had seen the book and had once more
exploded, and Cromwell hastened to stop Vaughan's activities in
a letter in which he hurriedly accepted the whole of the King's
opinion of Tyndale – a man 'replete with venomous envy, rancour
and malice' – and urged Vaughan never to profess a liking for
him again.[13] Nor was this mere device: all through, the idea of
using Tyndale had really been Vaughan's, as emerges clearly
enough from the fact that despite these instructions the agent
did not abandon the scheme. Immediately he took the line that
the King would have thought better of Tyndale if he had read the
book against More himself rather than rely on another man's
reading – a perceptive but tactless remark – and he kept in touch
with the reformer.[14] Evidently unable to absorb a straight order
'to desist and leave any further to persuade or attempt' Tyndale,
Vaughan was forwarding new works by him for presentation to

[10] Demaus, *Tyndale*, 273.
[11] *LP* v. 65; cf. Demaus, *Tyndale*, 272–4.
[12] Ibid. 274.   [13] Merriman, i. 335–9.
[14] Ellis, ii. II. 206–7 (*LP* v. 303).

the King as late as November 1531, though at this point Cromwell's reaction finally made him desist.[15]

It is at this point also that his correspondence with Cromwell becomes important to us. The Tyndale episode had shown how much more enthusiastic Vaughan was than his master for the cause of reform in religion, as well as the skill with which Cromwell had handled the King's attempt to try him out without sacrificing his awkward friend and servant. Vaughan was chastened to the extent of angrily rebutting the charges of heresy which he knew More was collecting against him and firmly asserting that he was 'neither Lutheran ne yet Tyndalyn'.[16] But ever since he had known that Cromwell had survived Wolsey's fall and stood fairly in the way of power with the King, he had been determined to make his friend serve the good cause to which, of course, he knew him to be inclined.[17] The Tyndale enterprise, though possibly in line with Cromwell's general intentions, had been a mistake, and Cromwell had avoided involvement in it. But there was a truth to be rescued from the fiasco, and late in 1531 Vaughan set about doing so. The mixture of innocent arrogance and earnest good will which characterized this peculiar merchant adventurer comes out well in a fragment he wrote, quite possibly at this time and probably for Cromwell's eyes, in which he excused the use of very plain speech by honesty of purpose and the duty owed to higher powers.[18]

In November, Vaughan found a new way of promoting the reform, a way which undermines the other half of his claim to be a follower of neither Luther nor Tyndale. He had discovered Robert Barnes and gone overboard for him. In fact, he sent a second copy of Barnes's book for fear that the first had gone astray, the messenger, 'to pick a thank', possibly having delivered it to the duke of Norfolk.[19] How he could contemplate with such

[15] *LP* v. 533.

[16] BM, Galba B. x, fos. 23–5 (*LP* v. 574).

[17] In October 1529 he anxiously enquired how Cromwell stood in 'this sudden overthrow of my lord your master' and offered 'any service in the world which I may do for you' (Ellis, ii. II. 171); in the following February he was relieved to know that all was well (*LP* iv. 6196).

[18] *LP Add.* 703. This reads like a preface intended for some piece of moralizing advice.

[19] SP 1/68, fos. 56–7 (*LP* v. 533). The book was Barnes's *Supplication unto King Henry VIII*, on which see W. D. J. Cargill-Thompson in *Transactions of the Cambridge Bibliographical Society*, iii (1960), 133–42.

equanimity the possibility that a notoriously Lutheran work with a covering letter to Cromwell might have reached the duke whose conservatism in religion was well known and who had no cause to encourage the rise of Cromwell, passes understanding; but then he thought it right that a book of which he himself said that the author quite probably 'shall seal it with his blood' should be presented by Cromwell to the King. Cromwell seems to have been able to prevent this disaster, but he had to listen to sage advice from this incompetent meddler in affairs.

I could flatter [wrote Vaughan] as the world many times doth, specially princes, not that I know any man so to do but that man's nature known and his frailness is easy to conject that with the regard of a prince, his power and might to advance, he is soon overthrown and easily caught in this kind of evil.

That Vaughan of all people should warn Cromwell not to take good fortune for granted was really a bit much. In his turn, Cromwell was to be no flatterer of princes:

Who seeth not that he that is an evil counsellor to a prince is an evil counsellor to a realm? If it be sin to be an evil counsellor to one man, what abomination, what devilish and horrible sin is it to be a flatterer or an evil councillor to a prince?

So do not hesitate: 'How good a deed should you do to help that Dr Barnes might declare the opinion of his book before the King's majesty!' Vaughan himself believed Barnes to be right and warned that no one could stop the advance of truth: 'heaven and earth shall sooner perish than one iota of God's Word (Christ being thereof witness) shall fail'. If Barnes was wrong, God would deal with him.

Cromwell's reaction to this effusion was so patient as to suggest that, extravagant though Vaughan's notions of a councillor's functions were, they yet touched an answering chord in the minister's mind. From Vaughan's next letter it appears that his friend and master confined himself to a warning to avoid any association with Protestant reformers; he hinted that George Constantine, a suspect then being investigated by Lord Chancellor More, might bring trouble to Vaughan. All this Vaughan shrugged off, with a degree of assurance which argues confidence both in his chances of proving his innocence and in Cromwell's good offices.[20] No doubt Constantine, fearful for his family and frightened of More, would fling accusations about 'rather than be tied by the leg with a cold and hard iron like a beast'. It would be better for the King 'to look to these kinds of punishment which in my poor opinion threateneth more hurt to the realm than those that [cause] his ministers to execute the same tortures and punishments do think or conject'. Instead of taking fright himself, he urged Cromwell to advise Henry to cease trusting 'to other men's policies which threateneth in my opinion the weal of the realm'. To Vaughan, Cromwell's policies were the right ones and his triumph in the King's Council the essential condition of sound reform. He claimed to have told him this before, though perchance Cromwell had not listened. 'But tarry awhile,' went on this unworldly adviser, 'and you shall be learned by experience; I see it begin already.' Not that he was a Lutheran looking for toleration to practise subversion. Only, the King must learn that repression will not kill the truth: people will continue dissatisfied until Henry would 'fatherly and lovingly reform the clergy of his realm'. His own loyalty need never be called in doubt. The one thing that troubled him was the story, allegedly spread by More, that Cromwell had come to regret ever befriending such an heretic as he was. He hoped he would not lose 'a most dear friend and special good master of you', but even if Cromwell had really turned against him he would never 'turn my heart from you from whom I have received far greater pleasures than these displeasures'. For himself, he would be all right, 'being right able par tout, as the Frenchman sayeth, to get my living'.[21]

Cromwell did not turn against him: in May, Vaughan could express his relief at receiving a 'friendly and rather fatherly' piece of reassurance.[22] But Cromwell cannot have remained entirely easy about this stream of incriminating letters crossing the narrow seas. As his policy was to prove, he did indeed share some of his friend's views on the reform of the clergy and of religion, and after reading these letters about Tyndale and Barnes he came increasingly to favour Lutheran ideas and propagandists. But he knew that such matters could not go for-

[20] BM, Galba B. x, fos. 23–5 (*LP* v. 574), 9 Dec. 1531.
[21] Vaughan's use of French may have been a private joke between him and Cromwell. A few years earlier he had sought Cromwell's help in his efforts to learn the language (*LP* iv. 5459).
[22] BM, Galba B. x, fo. 9 (misplaced by *LP* v. 247 into 1531).

ward in the urgent and unsubtle manner demanded by Vaughan, and he seems therefore to have decided to turn Vaughan's energies into safer channels. Let him prove his usefulness to the King by writing about the thing on which he was expert: the problems of the English cloth-exporters at Antwerp. By 22 January 1532, Vaughan had completed a memorial on the subject. Cromwell's pressure to get on with it had resulted in many imperfections, but he was forwarding it for presentation to the King. At the same time, he did not wish his name to be mentioned in connection with it: since it was highly critical of his Flemish colleagues, it would be very awkward for him if he were revealed as its author, and he warned that if it were decided to employ the German Hanse in order to outflank the Netherlanders he would not be the right person for the negotiations. In commercial matters he showed the kind of cautious common sense which he would have done well to apply to his other affairs.[23] By March he felt rather better about the pamphlet and urged that the scheme he had put up for overcoming embargoes and sharp practices in the Netherlands market should be submitted to Parliament so that the Commons might know the damage being done to English interests.[24] Unfortunately we do not know what it was he proposed; his memorial should probably be identified with his 'articles. . .for a common wealth' filed away among Cromwell's papers but otherwise lost.[25]

In the spring of 1532 Vaughan lapsed into silence on the issues of the day; in any case, after More's resignation in May and the emergence of the new policy, he had reason to think that his advice and urgings had been heeded at last. In truth, of course, Cromwell had always meant to pursue reform as soon as he could gain control; his patience with Vaughan was that of a friend, not of a disciple. But the active mind and conscience of this evangelical merchant could not remain at rest for ever, and

[23] LP v. 739, 753.
[24] BM, Galba B. x, fo. 6v (LP v. 870). On the strength of this paper, Mc-Conica (English Humanists, 134–5) has asserted that Vaughan was 'recruited' into Cromwell's staff of people who were contributing 'to the high political discussions in his clientele'. It should be apparent by now that Vaughan needed no recruiting, but the one paper he is known to have written was on the subject of trade. 'Articles' meant proposals not a formal treatise, and 'for a common wealth' was a formula readily applied to anything with an economic content.
[25] Above, p. 14.

on 7 December 1534 he reverted to his old habit of complicating a letter of reports and news with massive reflections on Cromwell's duty in his high office.[26] He feared that Cromwell was allowing the routine burdens of government to deflect him from his higher tasks, and he spoke some sense on the danger of a man trying to do everything himself. He noted that the population of the Netherlands was probably not far short of England's, 'though England be somewhat greater'; yet a man like the bishop of Palermo, the leading councillor there, had not 'half the business, no not the tenth part, that you have', and the same was true of chief councillors elsewhere. No doubt this 'argues a great lack of justice abroad' when ministers there did not attend to the affairs of the subject as Cromwell did in England, but there were at least two dangers in Cromwell's assiduous involvement in private persons' business. The King lost the advantage of having so notable a councillor when he was burdening himself and dulling his wits 'with the continual travail of common causes'. Such a councillor, on the other hand, 'by overmuch paining his body and cumbering his wits. . .hasteth his death before his time'. Cromwell should think about fundamentals, not exhaust himself in dealing with every man's affairs.

In particular, Vaughan urged that Cromwell should 'help that justice may be had and done in every borough, town and city, and that thereby people be led to live in an order, and in the love, fear and dread of the prince and his laws'. He had in mind a reform of the judiciary which would cause all disputes and offences to be judged where they occurred, so that no one would be compelled to seek justice 300 miles from home and perhaps be unable to obtain it 'but by favour of corrupt ministers, officers and servants'. In this way, Cromwell would prolong his life, being 'vigilant in how the gifts of God be great in you and have brought you to a high authority'.

Half your years be spent;[27] look therefore upwards and weary not yourself so much in the work as though it should ever endure. . .Help the common causes of the realm, for the other be more hurtful than you are sometimes brought in hand, and be but trifles. What a fool am I thus to write when, I think, you remember all these things; but how much more a fool

26 SP 1/87, fos. 97–9 (*LP* vii. 1515).
27 Cromwell was about fifty at this time!

when it would be doubted how you would take such pre-
sumptuous counsels. But doubt who will: my doubt is past.
I have proved you in greater and harder than these and have
found you a glad and gentle hearer.

The recognition of all this did him some credit, after the Tyndale
affair. He concluded that if his assessment was wrong he would
have to suppose that Cromwell's wits were failing: 'for I do know
that never have men greater need of assured and friendly counsel
than when they sit in authority, their hearts sore cumbered with
affections and their eyes altogether blinded'.

Vaughan was right: Cromwell put all this down to old friendship, and the merchant's career prospered. His advice, too, was
this time sound enough: Cromwell was certainly overworking,
especially in his determination to listen to every man's troubles.
Whether he would have done more for 'the common causes of
the realm' if he had managed to reserve his time for them is
another question; at least it may be said with assurance that
Vaughan's vague proposals for improving the local provision of
justice – which would have added yet more officers to supervise
and more appeals from inferior jurisdictions – would have done
nothing to reduce the pressure on the minister's time. Vaughan
wrote no more pieces of advice that we know of. Cromwell, who
had recently secured him the preferment of an absentee clerkship
in the Chancery, once again used his services according to his
best skills when he got him appointed undertreasurer of the
mint.[28] But clearly his old friend and speaking conscience was
more than a client. To Vaughan, Cromwell represented the
nation's hopes of reform – reform of religion and of the particular
ills of the commonwealth. Though he wrote almost nothing on
the latter, Cromwell evidently valued his opinion where it was
expert, probably more than he valued his unsolicited advocacy
of Protestantism. Vaughan was no Erasmian and no member of
any team: he was one of the many people with whom Cromwell
talked about fundamental issues and to whom he gave a patient
and attentive hearing.

Stephen Vaughan was an old friend of Cromwell's; Thomas
Starkey, the most considerable thinker in that circle, introduced

[28] *Tudor Revolution*, 197, 260 n.2.

himself as a virtual stranger early in 1535. An Oxford man of strongly humanist leanings, Starkey had spent most of the years since about 1525 on the continent, mostly in Reginald Pole's household.[29] Two things in particular qualified him for service in the reformed polity: as he told Cromwell, he had always planned to use his intellectual training in practical affairs, and he had objected to the papal primacy long 'before this matter was moved here in our country'.[30] His approach to government was, however, delayed by his decision to add a knowledge of the civil law to his equipment in arts and theology, an enterprise not completed until the first half of 1534 at the earliest.[31] It may be also that he was further delayed by ignorance of what was going forward in England. In July 1534 he had a letter from John Mason, then on embassy in Spain, which among other things told him the news from home.[32] '*Papam non agnoscimus*. That I am sure you know. Every man swears now *in verba Regis et Reginae; qui nolunt, turriti statim fiunt.*' Among those in the Tower were Fisher and More. As for the Nun of Kent, Mason supposed that Starkey had heard of her execution but would give the details if he had not. Though Mason, rather indiscreetly, went on to wonder 'what end this tragedy will come to', Starkey may well have realized that his time had come. He wound up his affairs at Padua and made for England, uninvited, unrecruited, so far unacquainted

---

[29] Starkey's life is sufficiently recounted in Zeeveld, *Foundations*, though there are some errors.

[30] *England in the Reign of Henry VIII*, ed. S. J. Herrtage (London, E.E.T.S. 1878), x, xli [hereafter cited as Herrtage].

[31] Zeeveld, *Foundations*, 81, 87. Zeeveld's supposition (pp. 87–90) that Starkey was active in government service before 1534 rests on error. The so-called opinion on the Divorce, dated April 1533 by *LP* vi. 414(i), could have been written at any time since 1531 and was clearly a private exercise; there is no evidence that it was ever sent to the King. The fragment, ibid. (iii), used by Zeeveld to link his argument, is quite irrelevant in the context. As for the idea that Starkey sat on Cranmer's divorce commission, this is simply nonsense. It is not quite clear how Zeeveld supposes that the identification of 'Dr [John] Hughes', a well-known canonist of the day, with Starkey got into Burnet's *History of the Reformation*, since he has Burnet correcting his book in 1816, a century after his death; in any case, there are no grounds for accepting this mysterious interposition. Starkey is vouched for at Paris, Avignon and Padua between January 1532 and December 1534, and never in England. Besides, if he had been so closely involved in the Divorce from 1533, would he have been unknown to Cromwell in 1535?

[32] Ellis, ii. II. 54–9, there misdated 1535. The correct date is adopted in *LP* vii. 945.

in high places, all of which he proved by lodging on arrival –
about 12 December 1534 – at the house of Lady Salisbury, his
previous patron's mother. Starkey came to seek employment, not
because employment was already waiting for him.[33]

On the other hand, he knew well enough how to achieve his
purpose. Almost immediately after his arrival, he wrote to Cromwell, preferring (as he said) the use of a letter because he knew
that Cromwell was always excessively besieged at audience time.
'Being to you a stranger and almost unknown,' he wrote briefly.
After spending 'many years in the study of letters' and attaining
some proficiency in 'the law of God and the law of man', he
sought an opportunity to apply his learning 'to some use and
profit of my country', and since the King now seemed 'set to the
restitution of the true common weal' he hoped that Cromwell
might make it possible for him to 'help thereunto'.[34] The approach
was well chosen: Cromwell was sufficiently intrigued to summon
the writer and discover more about him. Starkey went off with
instructions to explain his intentions more fully, instructions
which fortunately for us he again fulfilled in a letter because it
was so difficult to find Cromwell at sufficient leisure for a proper
discussion.[35] He now explained why he put his trust in Cromwell:
the minister's present power was admittedly part of the reason,
but chiefly he was moved by what he heard of Cromwell's 'goodness in setting forward at honest purposes', by the report of
Cromwell's wisdom and virtues, and by his own experience of
Cromwell's 'singular humanity and gentleness' during their interview. He again and at greater length explained his qualifications,
evidently with an eye to giving Cromwell ammunition for
advocacy with the King, and also assured the minister of his

---

[33] He announced his arrival in a letter of Dec. 13th (*LP* viii. 132). Zeeveld,
Foundations, 91, supposed that he came as Lady Salisbury's chaplain, but
there is no evidence for this at all. Lady Salisbury's house was at Dowgate
in London (not Howgate, as Zeeveld repeatedly has it). Starkey continued
to lodge there long after he had gained employment with the King (*LP*
ix. 981), which indicates that he simply used the place as a hotel.

[34] Herrtage, lxvii–viii. Despite Herrtage this is no draft but the first item in
the extant Starkey–Cromwell correspondence.

[35] This letter (ibid. ix–x) must have been written in late January 1535. 'The
reading of this scroll' here refers to the letter itself, not to an enclosure,
as Zeeveld supposed (*Foundations*, 142–3), an error which had misled me
before this (e.g. *Proc. Brit. Acad.* liv [1968], 169). Starkey's paper on
Aristotle, which Zeeveld identified with this imaginary enclosure, was
produced later (below, p. 49).

undying loyalty to the man who would secure him promotion into the King's service.

Cromwell thought well of his new acquaintance and moved with speed. By February 15th, Starkey had been appointed a King's chaplain and was at court; his career of counselling in the public service was under way.[36] Henry had immediate use for his new chaplain: it was the King himself who thought to obtain Pole's support for his new order, and Starkey was soon involved in the long correspondence with Padua.[37] He displayed a characteristic enthusiasm which nearly proved disastrous to him when Pole at last, in his book on the unity of the Church, revealed his unshakable attachment to the papacy. This business engaged Starkey, but it can hardly be described as the service to the common weal which he had hoped to do; for this he found better opportunity in his relations with Cromwell whose servant he formally never was.

Those relations are interesting because they appear to have had no specifically political purpose but to have rested essentially on a kind of academic dialogue. Cromwell took an early opportunity both to impress Starkey and to get a piece of work out of him: at one of those general discussions described by Oliver, as the minister was holding forth 'to the great admiration of all such as were with you present', he asked the humanist scholar to produce a resumé of 'what thing it is after the sentence of Aristotle and the ancient peripatetics that commonly among them is called policy'. Starkey used a part of his manuscript on the state – the book we know as *The Dialogue between Pole and Lupset* – which he dressed up for the occasion in the form of an address to 'a rude multitude and ignorant, desiring to live in true policy', not perhaps the most tactful response to the request, though it enabled Cromwell to see that Starkey could write the sort of thing that was required in propaganda pamphlets.[38] This scene is revealing enough; even more instructive are the exchanges

[36] *LP* viii. 218.

[37] That the idea was Henry's was later stated by Starkey to the King himself: 'it pleased your highness, shortly after I was admitted to your grace's service, to commit unto me the writing of your commandment and request to Mr Rainold Pole in the most weighty cause which of many years hath been attempted in this your realm' (SP 1/105, fo. 119 [*LP* xi. 156]).

[38] SP 1/89, fos. 181–6 (*LP* viii. 216[2]); there is no no. 216(iii) as per Zeeveld, *Foundations*, 143 n.1, and the foliation there cited is one that belonged to an earlier binding.

of April 1535 around a manuscript of Starkey's now lost which formed the germ of his *Exhortation to the People*.[39] On that occasion Cromwell not only tested his new acquaintance's learning and ability but also proved himself fully Starkey's equal at this sort of learned argument. The evidence is patchy and has been worse muddled by editors of calendars and modern historians; I propose here to tell the story as connectedly as possible, rather than drift from one confusing letter to another.

Cromwell had sized his man up instantly; the scholar proved a good deal slower at understanding the minister. His exercise on Aristotle carried an air of condescension, but a later conversation opened Starkey's eyes. On that occasion Cromwell lent Starkey a book – 'your book', Starkey called it, leaving us to guess whether we have here a volume from Cromwell's shelves or a lost composition from his pen – and in returning it Starkey used language which recalls Harvey's opinion. Cromwell's discourse, full of intellectual curiosity joined to 'many profound and deep considerations of God, of authority and of other politic worldly things', had overwhelmed him with a sense of being specially favoured: surely, being thought worthy of 'such a loving and wise conversation' proved Cromwell's high opinion of him. But after this characteristic display of scholar's self-centredness, he went on to say that he had known such abilities as Cromwell's only in a few men who 'wholly have been given all their life to the study of letters which you never have made any great profession', and thus encouraged he expounded at length some ideas of his own on the foundations of secular and spiritual politics. It was in that conversation apparently that Cromwell emphasized the importance of moderation, of the middle way, in political analysis which struck such an answering chord in the adiaphoristic Starkey. Even as he wrote this letter he was also putting together a 'little scroll' setting out his beliefs on the nature of the polity; it was out of this that his *Exhortation* was to grow. 'Fearing to trouble you with such trifles', he had delayed delivery, but an experience with Henry changed his mind. The King, it would seem, had cross-questioned his chaplain on much the same mat-

---

[39] The evidence consists of three letters of Starkey's the correct order of which is SP 1/89, fos. 179–80; 95, fos. 59–60; 89, fos. 177–8 (*LP* viii. 216[1], 575, 215). The approximate date of these exchanges is given by *LP* viii. 575 which refers to the troubles with Father Reynolds (April 1535).

ters with particular reference to the arguments to be used against Father Reynolds's papalism, but Starkey's answer had not pleased: Henry had disapproved it on the grounds that 'it was not drawn out of Scripture'. So Starkey decided to work up his scroll, to get Cromwell to read and criticize it, and to ask for it to be shown to the King since it would prove that Starkey's opinion rested both on Scripture and on 'the deepness of philosophy'.[40] Starkey had learned that Henry had his doubts about him: hence this attempt to restore his position.

There is no sign that the 'scroll' ever came to the King's eyes, but Cromwell read it with care and offered serious criticism. To this Starkey listened with a new respect: carefully reconsidering the scroll (now become an oration and a book), he concluded that Cromwell was quite right. He was no longer surprised at this: 'even like as you have done in all other things which at any time it hath pleased you to talk with me, ever touched the string and knot of the matter, inasmuch that of your communication I have gathered more fruit of truth than I have of any other man living since I came here to my country'. Cromwell had cut to the heart of the question: 'this mean is not put at large which you require;' and Starkey was the more impressed because other people with whom Cromwell had discussed the book's thesis had strongly disapproved the author's lack of commitment to either extreme. Of course, despite his agreement that the middle way must, as Cromwell asked, be brought out even more, Starkey found an excuse for not having done so from the beginning: he had been trying to address 'the people' at large and felt that such fine points of political philosophy had to be put crudely and inadequately to that audience. However, he ended with a song of praise on the *via media* which in effect reappeared in the *Exhortation*, and with a fervent hope that the King could be induced to institute it in England.

This draft, now lost, formed the basis for Starkey's *Exhortation*, the only one of his writings to be published in his life time. It was so published because Cromwell wanted it out, and he certainly valued it in part at least for its use as propaganda: he had some difficulty in getting Starkey to add to his chosen subject of

[40] Zeeveld, *Foundations*, 147, errs in thinking that Henry had read the 'scroll'; Starkey's letter (SP 1/92, fo. 60) makes it quite plain that there had been only a verbal exchange with the King.

unity the theme, required by policy, of obedience.[41] But Starkey's letters can leave no doubt that Cromwell's interest in the book stemmed fundamentally from its exposition of ideas which he himself had put to Starkey: it was an engaged and intellectual interest. The letters also demonstrate the real relationship between the two men, which was that of intellectual equals, fellow-thinkers debating political ideas, rather than that of employer and employee, of the organizer and the writer of propaganda. The *Exhortation* was not commissioned; it grew out of their arguments and the concurrence of their opinions, and its use as propaganda came as an afterthought.

This point matters greatly if we are to understand the parts played by both men in the planning of reform. For Starkey had ideas not only on the structure of the true polity but also on the measures required if that polity was to become a true common-wealth. He produced two major writings on the subject. One was the famous *Dialogue between Pole and Lupset*, virtually completed before he returned to England. In this he set out the main lines of social reform which he wished to see pursued, and I have shown before this that the *Dialogue* played its part in the work of the Cromwellian reform group.[42] Perhaps even more significant was the second treatise, cast in the form of a long letter addressed (and quite possibly despatched) to Henry VIII in about July 1536, because here the programme sprang directly out of what had been happening in England. Unlike the *Dialogue*, it was therefore intended to advocate immediate practical policies. Starkey wrote it after reading Pole's *De Unitate* and seemingly before he realized how dangerously Pole's 'treason' had undermined his own position with the King. In consequence he was exceptionally frank and urgent.[43]

Starkey advised the King that his revolutionary policy needed to be shown to be both peaceful and constructive; he emphasized that one of the main ends to be pursued was that of setting an example to other kings and realms. Mid-1536, he argued, offered exceptional opportunities on two grounds: one was that the removal of Anne Boleyn had ended a situation in which 'few acts could proceed by the conjecture of wise men which might be durable with our posterity', the other that the increase in the

---

[41] *Policy and Police*, 193.   [42] *Proc. Brit. Acad.* liv (1968), 165ff.
[43] SP 1/105, fos. 119–40 (*LP* xi. 156), partly printed in Herrtage, xlviii–lxiii.

Crown's revenues from ecclesiastical first fruits and monastic lands had made a liberal policy possible. Accordingly, he asked for two things intended to restore stability in the realm. In the first place, he urged Henry to name the Lady Mary as his successor – 'the flower of all ladies and the very glass and image of all virtue and nobility' – at least until the Seymour marriage had produced issue.[44] To this bold initiative he joined an equally bold condemnation of the use of violence in establishing the revolution. He reminded Henry that he had always been against severe punishments and had once ventured to warn the King against dealing extremely with More and Fisher because extremity would hinder 'the truth of the cause' and get the English Reformation a bad name.[45] Starkey seems to have thought that more peaceful means would have disarmed opposition; which was one opinion that Cromwell, however much he may have wished to avoid killing More, cannot have shared. One wonders what Henry (if he ever saw it) made of his chaplain's gratuitous praise of the disinherited Mary, of those regrets for great men needlessly destroyed by the violent ways adopted to secure the revolution, or indeed of the slip of the pen which called the bishop of Rome pope![46]

However, Starkey's main purpose touched the possibility that the new wealth of the Crown might be used to remedy the ills of society. He set out a basic principle:

> Your highness most clearly seeth how the wealth of all princes
> hangeth chiefly of the wealth of their subjects, and how
> penury ever breedeth sedition, and how the heaping of
> treasure without liberality hath always brought in ruin and
> destruction of every commonwealth.

Starkey was, in fact, a primitive Keynesian who argued that the condition of the people was best remedied by pumping in government money 'to the comfort of them which shall be profitable citizens living in some honest exercise in this your commonalty', and he particularly argued for the support of the gentry's military training and the scholars' educational needs. Monastic funds, hitherto used for the support of the idle few, should be turned to public and general use; and he held it proper to break the wills of founders who had intended to serve the needs of the common-

[44] fo. 121v.   [45] fos. 122v–123r.   [46] fo. 124r.

wealth (through monks' devotions) in ways which the present age no longer considered valid. The lengthy discussion of this point is interesting: it throws light on the principled rejection of the monastic ideal, quite separate from disgust at its modern perversion and entirely independent of desire for wealth, which prevailed in Cromwell's circle.[47] One may well call these views Erasmian; at any rate, they rested on a reasoned understanding of the secular needs of the nation seen as a religious obligation on rulers. Having justified the diversion of the newly acquired funds, Starkey set out the particular problems requiring attention: underpopulation, unused land, decay of towns.[48] These points are familiar from his dialogue, as is his emphasis on the need to encourage marriage and procreation, though he now added that the King could choose either to reduce the number of priests or permit clerical marriage – either way he would produce the much needed increase in numbers. There are tenuous signs, in fact, of moves towards permitting the marriage of the clergy, though Henry very soon quashed all such – to him simply disgusting – proposals.[49] As for the exploitation of the land, this would be best achieved by leasing it in relatively small parcels to active occupiers rather than add it to the already overlarge, and therefore inefficient, estates of great men.[50]

The last section of this tract switches to a consideration of the supremacy (which Starkey justified by means of a competent review of papal history)[51] and the King's best way of exploiting it. The theme is unity; the suggestion is a reduction in the amount of contentious preaching. As usual, we get a heavy stress on 'the mean'. All this familiar matter culminates in yet another version of the basic need to prove the success of the English Reformation to the world. Discord, economic weakness, and loss of learning form no encouragement to others to do likewise; and Starkey points to the example of Germany, so lately a model to thinking men but now only a dispiriting indication of what can happen when a nation prefers extreme and violent courses to peaceful moderation. In his attack on too much preaching, Starkey dis-

---

[47] fos. 126–8. [48] fos. 129v–132r.
[49] Policy and Police, 252, 256.
[50] The insistence that no one should possess land who did not personally occupy it occurs elsewhere in the ideas of Cromwell's advisers; see below, p. 101.
[51] fos. 132v–134r.

tanced himself very much from Cromwell's Protestant allies – from Latimer, Barnes and Crome – but he was closer to government thinking at this time, for serious steps to bring the pulpit under better control had started early in 1536.[52]

This interesting tract represents evidently just the sort of thing that Cromwell expected to get from the thinkers with whom he involved himself. Starkey was no recruit of his. On the contrary, the scholar had come on his own initiative, seeking advancement to that position of influence which was advised by the brand of humanism to which he belonged. He had sought it by approaching the man, now at the top, of whose interest in matters of the mind he had heard encouraging news. Cromwell found Starkey congenial and freely discussed both fundamentals and details with him. The signs are strong that he hoped for a rational analysis of practical problems from one who laid claim to the ability to provide it and had offered some proof in writing. In the outcome, Cromwell may have been both satisfied and disconcerted when he got so much good advice of which such large parts were manifestly not practicable in the world of Henry VIII and the early Reformation. There is nothing to suggest that Starkey ever made any impact on the King he had come to serve, and the fiasco of the negotiations with Pole – the one enterprise in which Starkey engaged on Henry's explicit instructions – must have ended what influence he might have had at court. But Cromwell, who protected yet another friend against the consequences of a political error of the first magnitude, argued, propounded and listened – and 'overshadowed our greatest clerks'.

Vaughan was in Cromwell's service before the days of power and left it for the King's when Cromwell became great; Starkey never belonged to Cromwell's official family. Richard Morison, on the other hand, became Cromwell's servant after the minister had reached the heights and remained so till the end. How and when he entered service is curiously difficult to establish, partly because of his deplorable habit of rarely dating his letters. Before 1533 his history is still obscure and not much illumined by those who have written on it,[53] but he was in Italy from about 1532. Soon in

[52] *Policy and Police*, 241–6.
[53] Zeeveld, *Foundations*, 27, 73–4; C. H. Cooper, *Athenae Cantabrigienses*, i. 143.

dire financial straits and without a useful patron (his then master, Thomas Winter, Wolsey's bastard son, being himself in difficulties), he started looking for betterment. In October 1533 he tried Cranmer whom he had met once or twice, though he did not expect the archbishop to remember him.[54] At this point he lived at Venice; soon after he joined Pole's household at Padua where he found bare shelter but neither patronage nor hope of financial security. About a year later we find his first two surviving letters to Cromwell, and they pose problems. Both are dated from Padua, one on October 26th and the other on October 27th, and both have been assigned to 1534.[55] There is in itself nothing improbable in a man ensuring thus against the accidents of the posts, but the two letters are so different in tone that the dating becomes very unlikely. The first is unquestionably that of a man who seeks acquaintance and favour; it was written by someone manifestly unknown to Cromwell. The second offers advice which in a stranger would be extremely impertinent: Cromwell is to banish rather than execute the enemies of the commonweal and to remember that a consenting obedience is a better foundation for the state than a forced acquiescence. Though signed 'tui favoris sitissimus' it is addressed to the secretary and councillor as 'patrono suo plurimum honorando'.[56] Thus the two letters cannot have been written on consecutive days. The date of the first must be 1534 since in earlier years Morison was not at Padua, and the second therefore belongs to 1535.[57]

Between, therefore, October 1534 and October 1535, Morison had achieved a status which enabled him to call Cromwell his patron, though formally, it appears, Winter remained his master until he returned to England.[58] In April 1536, Morison called himself Cromwell's 'scholasticus' – his scholar who was bound to him and received some maintenance from him.[59] In fact, Morison had by then thought of Cromwell as his master for something like six months; he had no difficulty in serving two such when one of them was the ineffectual Winter. In October 1534 he had remarked that his friends had advised him to seek promotion with

[54] *LP* vi. 1582.   [55] *LP* vii. 1311, 1318.
[56] BM, Nero B. vi, fos. 151–2; this detail is omitted in *LP* vii. 1318.
[57] This disposes of Zeeveld's remarks (*Foundations*, 93–4) on Morison's courage in advising Cromwell on the fate of More and Fisher. Both were dead when Morison wrote.
[58] *LP* x. 661.   [59] Ibid. 600.

Cromwell; a year later he wrote a letter to Starkey in which he inquired after his master's welfare in terms which leave no doubt that Cromwell was intended. The chances are that he was in service by late August 1535 when he wrote at length to report the shock experienced in Italy at the news of More's and Fisher's deaths (the well-known *Paris Newsletter* reporting the event having reached that country'.[60] Morison was perfectly frank, as he always was, about the horror he heard on every side, but he went on to expound his advice on how the impression might best be eradicated. In fact, he was giving good advice on propaganda: Cromwell would do well to concentrate on the fact that More and Fisher had broken a trust and to use classical Roman precedents for the execution of great servants of the state who had afterwards turned against their proper allegiance. It is hard to suppose that this letter could have been written by anybody not in a formal and close relationship to the addressee. What is more, the advice was taken: the long propaganda letter which Cromwell sent to Gregory Casale in September essentially adopted the suggested tone of pained surprise that anyone should wish to defend persons who, however eminent in their day, had so ill requited the trust reposed in them.[61] Morison's first approach to Cromwell reached the minister just about the time that he first became acquainted with Starkey; no doubt he asked Starkey's opinion of this further suitor from Padua, and it was presumably Starkey's recommendation that altered Morison's fortunes. The letter of August 1535 also indicates for what purpose Cromwell originally received Morison into his service. He was not looking for a humanist adviser, but for an informant well placed to report. Morison was at first part of Cromwell's foreign intelligence service, and the possibility that he was intended to keep an eye on what was going on in Pole's group also cannot be discounted. In his later propaganda work Morison showed himself both well informed about Pole and exceptionally hostile to him.

It was this specific employment which also accounts most convincingly for the difficulties Morison experienced when in early 1536 he decided to return to England and make his fortune

---

[60] *LP* ix. 198. Zeeveld (*Foundations*, 94) calls this letter 'highly critical', but he seems to have misread Morison's difficult Latin. In fact, Morison did not criticize but discussed ways of putting the executions in a better light.
[61] Merriman, i. 427–31.

at the fountain head. This is a confused story – confused by
Morison – which needs to be clarified if Cromwell's attitude is to
be understood. Poverty, as usual with Morison at this time, lay
behind his decision: on 18 February 1536 he acknowledged that
without a gift from Starkey he could not have survived.[62] On the
29th he hoped for money from Cromwell and hinted that he
would welcome a summons home.[63] But he decided to pretend to
his friends that it was Cromwell who wanted him in England
and in his household, so far a manifest lie, for late in March he
reiterated his earlier veiled request through the intermediacy of
Starkey.[64] Starkey had told him how impressed Cromwell was by
his letters: the minister had spontaneously commented on their
excellence before dinner and taken the opportunity to praise
Morison at table, in the general conversation. If Cromwell would
call him home, would Starkey make sure that travel money was
sent? On April 12th Morison wrote to Cromwell explicitly requesting a call home, and to Starkey wondering if there was any
chance of such a summons.[65] By early May he was at last preparing for the journey, and on the 22nd of that month he departed
from Italy.[66] Thus Cromwell had taken some persuading: Morison
worked hard for three months before he got the desired recall.
It would seem that much as the minister appreciated his new
servant's abilities he valued his presence best in Italy. At the same
time, it is, of course, true that it was Morison's scholarly abilities
– and the exceptional liveliness of his Latin letters – which
attracted Cromwell: he may not have sought a humanist reformer,
but he got one.

Unlike Vaughan, who denied his Protestant leanings so apparent to others, and Starkey who never showed any inclination to
Lutheranism, Morison was from the first a firm Protestant, a fact
which appears from all his writings. He also had some interest in
social reform, as his rather incompetent attempt to codify the
laws of England showed.[67] But of all Cromwell's young men he
was the only one who can be called a professional writer of
propaganda, a function in which he was extensively employed
from the moment he returned to England to the end of Crom-

[62] *LP* x. 321.
[63] Ibid. 372.
[64] Ibid. 660–1.
[65] Ibid. 418, 565.
[66] Ibid. 801, 961.
[67] *Proc. Brit. Acad.* liv (1968), 177–80.

well's ascendancy.[68] Cromwell judged his abilities shrewdly: here was an eager young scholar of little originality of mind, but with the liveliest pen of the day. Their personal relationship seems to have been close – a kind of courteous friendship based on mutual enjoyment of each other's company. Morison had from the first hoped for just such things. His initial approach to Cromwell had been intended to solve his problem of patronage, but once he had been accepted he had boldly praised Cromwell's achievement as the liberator of England from the papal yoke and proclaimed that all those with reform at heart expected great things from his government.[69] He nailed his colours to that mast with more reckless abandon than most, and after Cromwell's fall, though he managed to survive and made a successful diplomatic career under Henry VIII and Edward VI, he abandoned his scholarly ambitions and reformist notions. There are no known contacts with the 'groups' of Catherine Parr and the duke of Somerset who allegedly took over the reformist mantle from Cromwell. As he told Cromwell soon after he became a full member of the team: 'I am a graft of your lordship's own setting; if I bring forth any fruits I know who may claim them.'[70] And Cromwell showed little haste to pass him on to the King's service. A false rumour that he had been appointed to the Privy Chamber greatly embarrassed Morison in the middle of 1538,[71] and despite a broad hint that the reality would be welcome it was only late in 1539 that the promotion took place – pretty well just in time to equip Morison for survival in the disaster of 1540.[72]

Something about the relationship of the two men may be gathered from two letters which Morison wrote to Cromwell from court, round about July 1538.[73] They are in English, but with bits of Italian and Latin in them which Morison evidently knew would not only be understood but please. Naturally, they are full of Morison's artifice, but it sounds sincerely meant. Though of duty he ought to make all his letters 'givers of thanks unto your good lordship's more than fatherly goodness towards me', this particular letter was further forced from him 'by a lovely lady

[68] *Policy and Police*, 191–2, 201–7.   [69] *LP* vii. 1318; x. 372.
[70] SP 1/113, fo. 210 (*LP* xi. 1481).   [71] *LP* xiii. I. 1296.
[72] *LP* xiv. II. 572, p. 201; Morison was not yet of the Privy Chamber at the beginning of the year (ibid. I. 1296–7).
[73] SP 1/133, fos. 251–2, 253–4 (*LP* xiii. I. 1296–7).

called friendship' (friendship for Edmund Harvel). Appeals for
others, regrets about the Privy Chamber, public and personal
business mingle, and in the end Morison asks Cromwell to put
his signature to a letter on Morison's behalf to King's College,
Cambridge. Evidently Morison had some qualms because of the
rather injured way in which he had previously written about that
non-existent promotion, but he need not have feared.

> I was half afraid lest my letters wherein love and friend-
> ship took their pleasure and would give no place to reason
> and duty should somewhat have displeased your lordship.
> *Ma merce alla vostra bonta, gentil natura e singular' amore,*
> I found it much otherwise.

Cromwell had promptly signed the letter to Cambridge, a fact
which called forth truly ardent declarations of love (that is,
attachment): 'There is no benefit of yours but it lies lodged in the
best corner of my heart, never to be removed from thence but
when the whole house breaketh up.' Yet what most fervently
attached Morison to Cromwell (or so he said: and that he did so
signifies something about the minister) was the lord privy seal's
zeal for the gospel and the truth – more than any benefactions to
himself from one 'which alone hath changed my fortunes, unto
whom alone (God not forgotten) I may give all thanks'. The
Lutheran ambassadors, to whom Morison had talked, knew that
England owed her rescue from superstition and darkness to
Cromwell alone. They grant 'Christum tibi multa debere, etsi tu
illi omnia debeas'! And Morison is carried away by his advocacy
of Harvel's suit and by the friendship between them in a long
passage worth quoting at length:

> I might percase thrive better if I sued for fewer. I think not so.
> No, my prayer is that I may bind all my friends to your lord-
> ship, taking this as a right rule and trial of a friendship, to
> love ever where I had once good cause to love. I never desired
> to have him my friend that, once promoted, rather sought new
> friends than kept his old. As I refuse no new, so I will never
> willingly leave mine old. Friendship should be like a marriage,
> for better for worse, for richer for poorer, till death depart.
> They cannot be separated whom true amity knitteth. All men,
> my lord, in your case are in such taking that hard it shall be to

know who loveth and who feigneth. My rule never faileth: he that regardeth his old friends (my lord, your joy and comfort may be great that you almost alone of all men that ever were in your place have not forgotten your old knows) may well be taken of trust as one very apt and meet to build friendship upon.

'I swerve too much from my purpose' – as indeed he did. But he testified here to an important truth about Cromwell and his company. This was a group held together by personal loyalties, looking for both friendship, benefits and great doings from the man around whom they had gathered and who in his turn treated them on a footing of equality. They had come to him rather than been collected by him, and they were less an official body than a company of like-minded men, a source of mental refreshment and stimulation as well as of advice and memoranda, haphazardly brought together and always on their own initiative.

The Cromwellians, therefore, were men who came to Cromwell because they hoped to find in him both a fountain of patronage and the man who could be expected to do for the realm of England what they, in their various ways, believed should be done. This is what happened with Vaughan, Starkey and Morison; it is also easily demonstrated for others. None of the people whom McConica has described as 'recruited by Cromwell' in fact entered his ambience in precisely that way. Take Richard Taverner who from 1535 onwards certainly acted as Cromwell's chosen instrument for the dissemination of a humanist Protestantism.[74] McConica's account of his entry into service is sadly astray.[75] He notes that Taverner published in 1531 a translation of Erasmus' *Encomium Matrimonii* with its attack on clerical celibacy and that the preface offers thanks to Cromwell for rescuing the author from destitution. He also notes a letter allegedly written in 1532 in which Taverner, unknown to Cromwell, appeals

[74] John K. Yost, 'German Protestant Humanism and the Early English Reformation: Richard Taverner and official translation,' *Bibliothèque d'humanisme et Renaissance* xxxii (1970), 613–25. Yost shows that Taverner not only translated Lutheran works but used his translations of Erasmus, too, in order to advocate Protestantism. He disposes of McConica's view which makes Taverner (and Cromwell) non-Protestant humanists.
[75] McConica, *English Humanists*, 117–18.

for aid, an appeal which Cromwell answered by recommending the scholar to the King and getting the duke of Norfolk, of all people, to offer an annuity.[76] It is obvious that these letters were written in 1530 – late that year, since Cromwell is called councillor – and not after the decision to translate Erasmus' book. To McConica this book 'sealed the bargain' between the two men: 'it is impossible to doubt,' he says, 'from the preface that this particular work was chosen by Cromwell, or at least in consultation with him'. In fact, from that preface it is impossible to believe any such thing: Taverner says plainly that, trying to think of some way to repay Cromwell's kindness, he happened upon the work of Erasmus and decided to translate it.[77] He wished to publish it under Cromwell's 'noble protection', but he says not one word to suggest that Cromwell knew of the idea before Taverner had executed it. Like the rest, Taverner sought Cromwell's favour and protection, obtained it by displaying his talents, and once accepted was in due course used as those talents best suggested.[78]

William Marshall also started his translating enterprises on his own initiative but managed to interest Cromwell in them; he then, and seemingly not for some years, entered the minister's service.[79] As for John Rastell, another alleged recruit, there is no evidence that he was ever a servant of Cromwell's or got much of a hearing, only evidence that he bombarded Cromwell with

[76] *LP* v. 1762–3.

[77] See preface to *STC* 10492 (BM, C.95.a.28): 'Your daily orator. . .pondering with himself your gratuity [and] bounty towards him, began busily to revolve in mind how he again on his part might somewhat declare his fervent zeal and heart towards you; which he thus revolving, he suddenly (as God would) a certain epistle of Dr Erasmus, devised in commendation of wedlock, offered itself unto his sight. Which so soon as he began to read, he thought it a thing full necessary and expedient to translate it. . . Please it your goodness, right honourable sir, to accept this rude and simple translation of your servant, and ye so doing shall not a little encourage him to great things in time coming.'

[78] Taverner was in Cromwell's service until c. 1536 when the lord privy seal promoted him into the King's, though in such fashion as to maintain close contact. The office obtained for him was that of clerk of the signet (*Tudor Revolution*, 305–6), not, as is commonly stated (e.g. McConica, *English Humanists*, 183) clerk of the privy seal.

[79] *Policy and Police*, 186 n.2. There is no good evidence that Marshall, despite manifest earlier contacts, was fully in service before 1536 (*LP* xi. 325), and Audley's remarks about him in Sept. 1535 (*LP* ix. 358) suggest that he, who knew Cromwell well, did not know Marshall as Cromwell's servant.

advice and that in 1535 Cromwell thought him a suitable man for the hopeless task of proselytizing among the London Carthusians.[80] The pattern is the same throughout: men concerned about the state of the realm and reform in religion made their way to his gates and were received with varying degrees of alacrity. Interestingly enough, humanist scholars seem to have pleased better than that curious set of simple-minded and exalted autodidacts from London – Rastell, Armstrong, Gibson.[81] Some of these men became Cromwell's servants, some he placed with the King, some again he listened to without comment or favour. Certainly, he looked for propagandists; as certainly he was interested in anything that tended to reform and reformation.

Nor is there any mystery about this rush of reformers, humanist or civic. It is quite plain that Cromwell's mind was well known; from the first he was recognized as a man passionate for reform. As Rastell explained: he had leant to Cromwell from early in 1530 because he saw him inclined to good causes.[82] We have seen that by 1533 the group of talkers and writers at Padua knew that

---

[80] That Rastell was Cromwell's servant from about 1532 was stated by A. W. Reed, *Early Tudor Drama* (London, 1926), 22. Reed's method of alleging his sources is thoroughly inadequate, but I have, I think, tracked them and can find no evidence testifying to service, only that Rastell in his zeal for religion and the commonwealth tried to interest Cromwell in his notions. One idea at least may have been taken up (below, pp. 144–7). Reed also confused a book which Rastell hoped to get published with official approval with the 'charge at sessions' which he and some friends had drawn up and hoped to see enacted by Parliament. His book has for too long been treated as gospel.

[81] Rastell was a friend of Clement Armstrong's (Reed, *Drama*, 26) who in turn appointed Thomas Gibson as his executor (*Bulletin of the Institute of Hist. Research*, xxv [1952], 126). Rastell, Armstrong and Richard Gibson had long been closely acquainted through shared work in the Revels Office (S. Anglo, *Spectacle, Pageantry and Early Tudor Policy* [Oxford 1969], 164–7). Richard died early in 1534 (ibid. 261); it may be safely conjectured that Thomas Gibson, the pamphleteer, was a relative, perhaps a son. These men, who from the early 1530's shared a zeal for reform, evidently formed a clique, but Anglo (pp. 262–5), who was misled by A. W. Reed, is mistaken in supposing that they ever entered Cromwell's service or played an active part in government propaganda. Whether one shares Anglo's and Reed's loud regrets for the loss of happier days when the three friends, now so anxious to assist a revolution, painted scenery and produced ceremonial displays, may be a matter of taste; they themselves seem to have welcomed the opportunity to write against the pope and to clamour for reform.

[82] *LP* vii. 1073. Armstrong made the same point (below, p. 112). Evidently the London circle of reformers knew all about Cromwell.

there was a man governing England who would (as they saw it) serve their purpose. Demands for reform were ancient enough, and the scholars who have discovered the ancestry of those preachers of renewal in Wolsey's household and the Universities of the 1520's have made a point of weight. A whole generation of intellectuals was burning to better their world and looked for a leader. Wolsey had turned out to be quite useless to them – not only the outstanding representative of that clerical order which they deplored but rarely interested in translating casual speculation into reality. His fall promoted Thomas More who should have been able to head the great humanist – 'Erasmian' – awakening, but More proved another broken reed because he concentrated all his energies on the extirpation of heresy and the maintenance of the Church. Some at least of the intellectuals displayed their disappointment in him at the time of his destruction, though others more generously continued to regret the unhappy fate which had deprived England of his pre-eminent greatness. In Cromwell they found a man not only willing to listen and discuss but manifestly also willing and able to do so. For the Cromwell here described – the friend and equal of scholars – was, of course, only one side of the man; as important to the reformers was the man of inexhaustible energy, fertile device, and relentless execution. In Thomas Cromwell a sincere passion for reform combined with a singular ability to get things done.

That part of the reform which no doubt seemed paramount to him and his associates – the reform of Church and religion – does not here concern us, though we should always remember that everything they did was intended to contribute to an overriding purpose: the creation of a worthy, well-administered, well-satisfied realm pleasing to God. As Cromwell himself put it: 'My prayer is that God give me no longer life than I shall be glad to use mine office in edification and not in destruction.'[83] Everything he undertook was to help towards the realization of his vision of the true polity, and we need to remember how much of it he achieved in the short time allowed him. But though Cromwell, a mundane and pragmatic prophet, had his visions, he also knew the need for particular action. The vision called for the renovation of the whole community of England; the particular action reformed the details of the commonwealth. And to this work Cromwell brought

[83] Merriman, ii. 129.

not only determination and executive ability, but also some unusual knowledge and experience. The friend of humanists, the
student of Marsiglio and perhaps Machiavelli, the man who,
overshadowing our greatest clerks, urged the conciliatory doctrine
of the *via media* on professional scholars, was also an ex-soldier,
ex-merchant, common lawyer and close friend of leading London
capitalists.[84] No English statesman so far had brought such a
combination of gifts and connections to his task. As a reformer
he also had the invaluable habit of doing his homework. His
whole correspondence testifies to his passion for accurate and
comprehensive information; what he did might well offend and
even destroy existing interests, but it would do so knowingly.
There would be no ignorant tinkering. His papers and his actions
alike, as I have already said, demonstrate his attention to detail
and even to statistics. When he contemplated the imposition of a
tax he first decided 'to collect the names of all the wealthy men
in the realm, as well priests, merchants and others',[85] though one
fears that that census was never carried out; the purpose of his
parish registers was in great part to end such uncertainties by
creating a proper demographic record and to remove problems of
descent and ownership from the realm of speculation.[86] As a
thinker, planner, administrator and enforcer, Thomas Cromwell
was singularly well equipped to reform the commonweal. But
above all, he fully understood how alone reform could be brought
about in England. He knew that only Parliament could do it, and
he knew all about the use and management of that instrument.

[84] Cromwell's connection with the city of London – with such great men
there as Paul Withipoll and Richard Gresham – needs more study than I
can give it here; it appears well enough from his correspondence.
[85] *LP* xiv. I. 655.
[86] Gilbert Burnet, *History of the Reformation,* ed. N. Pocock (Oxford, 1865),
vi. 224.

4

THE INSTRUMENT

The historians of humanism and its social programme have curiously missed one of its central problems. How were all those bright ideas to be translated into action? The reformers wanted new laws, and in England this could only mean new parliamentary statutes. This fact produced complications of the most diverse kinds, both for reformers and historians, and while in the present state of knowledge I cannot pretend to resolve them all I think it very necessary to look closely at them. Humanist thinking on reform took much of its inspiration from continental sources, from people working in situations in which the standard specific – to counsel princes – seemed adequate. In all those discussions on the duty of scholars to take their advice into the world of power, the sole target aimed at is always the prince. Even Thomas More, who should have known better, takes it for granted in *Utopia* that the way to influence is the way to court and that nothing further is needed beyond straight access to the ear of the ruler. Now if the advice to be given touched only such things as the virtues of peace over war, a diplomacy based on creating a united Christendom, or the need to administer justice fairly – the rather obvious commonplaces of humanist advisory thought – talking to princes might indeed suffice. But More, for instance, showed himself well aware that the state of society demanded reforms which could come only by changing the laws of the realm, and in England, as he also knew perfectly well, kings did not change laws by themselves or make new ones. True, there were quite a few laws in existence which might remedy some of the evils complained of if only they were properly enforced; and proper enforcement was a task to be carried out by princes and their counsellors. But it was generally agreed that the existing good laws were not enough, and even those that might be approved would do better if freshly enacted. Kings of England could issue proclamations, and (as we shall see) very occasionally a minor reform could be initiated by those very limited instruments. Real change, however, was bound to rely on statute.

The standing of statute was high: time and again, respect for disconcerting change was demanded on the grounds that it had been agreed in Parliament.[1] There is no need to labour a sufficiently familiar point, but I may draw attention to one exchange because it involved Cromwell.[2] In 1535, when he was troubled about Bishop Gardiner's doubtful attitude, he found himself interrogating John Mores, receiver of Syon monastery, who admitted to having discussed fundamental questions concerning the supremacy with the bishop of Winchester. Mores said that he had tried to provoke Gardiner by suggesting that the papal primacy rested on the consent of General Councils, but Gardiner had parried this by accepting the authority of the Act of Parliament as discharging his conscience. Cromwell asked how Mores could have agreed with such a view: if the pope's claims rested on General Councils 'whereunto some affirm and hold opinion that the Holy Ghost be present', how could parliamentary statute overrule them? Mores readily followed this leading question:

Mine opinion concerning the General Council is than an Act of Parliament made in the realm for the common wealth of the same ought rather to be observed within the same realm than any General Council. And I think that the Holy Ghost is as verily present at such an act as it ever was at any General Council.

The Act of Supremacy, in his opinion, was 'as much for the common wealth of this realm as any act that ever was made before the King's time that now is'. He claimed to have opened the question with Gardiner because – 'as ye, Mr Secretary, best know' – it had been often raised 'in the Parliament House and taken amongst many there to be a doubt'. One result of the work of the Reformation Parliament was to end such doubts: divinely inspired or not, the Parliament's statutes now stood omnicompetently sovereign. Not only could they stand out against the canons of General Councils; they also ruled supreme against the King's own edicts. This point, as is well known, was made by Gardiner to Somerset in 1547 when he found it useful in his endeavour to resist religious changes put through by proclamation; it seems to be less well known that Cromwell affirmed the

[1] Cf. the orders to J.P.s, *Policy and Police*, 239.
[2] SP 1/92, fos. 68–70 (*LP* viii. 592[3]).

same principle to Thomas More when he warned him that no royal licence could dispense him from the Acts of Supremacy and Treason.[3]

The Act of Parliament was, then, a powerful instrument: once made, it commanded obedience of a virtually religious character, and more practically it had the whole weight of the common law's organs of enforcement behind it. The reformers who promoted particular ideas were well aware of all this, and Cromwell's papers are full of proposals for action by Parliament, or (perhaps more revealingly) requests that certain notions might be put through Parliament by the minister's organization. Rastell on one occasion sent Cromwell a paper proposing administrative action for the reform of the heresy laws, the printing of propaganda tracts, and a list of five projected statutes, three of them for law reform.[4] It was one of the peculiarities of the whole scene that until Cromwell found a seat for Richard Morison in the 1539 Parliament none of the people active in reform and associated with the government, himself excepted, had parliamentary experience – not even Thomas Elyot who, one might have supposed, belonged to the usual parliamentary classes.[5] Official and unofficial reformers concentrated on preparing matters for a Parliament which they knew only from outside, and thanks to the English constitution there was nothing else they could do. One finds straight lists of reforms asking that this or that be enacted;[6] one finds bills 'drawn and not put up for the Parliament House';[7] one finds draft bills which can be linked with actual legislation and others which can be shown to have failed in Parliament. As much as anything else, the study of reform in the 1530's is a study of parliamentary legislation – planned, attempted, achieved or lost.

How well reformers were aware of the need to go beyond the throwing out of bright ideas or the persuasion of princes appears in the fact that the most striking proposals of the day are found not in treatises and pamphlets (which usually diagnose trouble

---

[3] *Letters of Stephen Gardiner*, ed. J. A. Muller (Cambridge, 1933), 390–1; *More's Correspondence*, ed. Rogers, 541.

[4] SP 1/85, fos. 99v–100 (*LP* vii. 1043); and the lists in *LP* ix. 725, discussed below, p. 110.

[5] Elyot, too, first sat in 1539 (Lehmberg, *Elyot*, 132n.).

[6] E.g. *LP Add.* 754.

[7] SP 1/152, fos. 11–14 (*LP* xiv. I. 1064).

but rarely devise specific reforms) but in documents taking the shape of an Act of Parliament. The two schemes which have been printed, for a Court of Conservators of the Common Weal (to enforce social legislation) and for a Court of Centeners (to use surplus ecclesiastical wealth for the defence of the realm), both adopt this form.[8] Manifestly unfinished though they are, and manifestly not commissioned for actual introduction into Parliament, they yet evince evident knowledge of what would be required if such pet schemes should manage to attract favourable official attention. The bill 'not put up' in Parliament turns out, on inspection, to be simply a disguised pamphlet: a two-page address to the King poses the question why the modern Church should be so disastrously different from the primitive Church, decides that corrupting wealth is the only cause, and goes on to offer a statute fully written out which will remedy things by removing the source of corruption. There is nothing 'official' about this document which includes in the preamble of the suggested act conceits of the kind that unfortunately do not liven up real statutes;[9] this is the work of a private person with rather obsessional ideas and some legal expertise who just knew that the way to reform lay through statute and therefore used the form when he was really writing a piece of political advice. As a piece of real drafting, his 'act' leaves a good deal to be desired.

There was one exception to this general reliance on Parliament. Clement Armstrong, a bitter old man after years of trading and fewer years of dreaming of a better England, complained that reform was barred by the unwillingness of King and Lords to undertake it except on the recommendation of the Commons. And yet there sat in that House the very exploiters of the nation whom reform would put down: monopolistic merchants, accumulators of farms, enclosers and sheep-farmers, riggers of the food market. Add, he says, the lawyers there who live on the 'sin and mischief of the common people' and prosper by keeping disputes and

---

[8] Discussed below, pp. 139–41.

[9] SP 1/152, fo. 12: 'Yet since an act in part begun and brought to a full conclusion is of small force, efficacy or value; neither can it worthily be called a reformation that in the chief part thereof is left unperfect: no more than a painter may say he hath painted a man when he hath made all the parts of the body in due proportion, leaving the head, the most noble part thereof, undrawn or unshapen; or that a carpenter may say he hath made a ship when he hath left the helm or the stern unwrought...'

contention alive: and what do you expect?[10] Armstrong may have
been speaking from close vicarious experience, for Robert
Urmeston or Armstrong, the clerk of the Commons, may have
been his brother or at least a near relative;[11] but the statute book
with its laws against depopulation, for the rebuilding of towns,
for price control and law reform, shows how wrong he was – in
company with a good many later commentators – in supposing
that self-interest ruled everybody all the time. But he was right
in thinking that reform through Parliament was a difficult thing,
much more difficult than that conversion of princes on which
continental humanists relied. Still, there was no other way out,
and it is quite possible that it was Armstrong's contempt for
Parliament even more than his habit of thinking everybody but
himself corrupt and wrong that put him out of court for Cromwell: Armstrong was the one prolific writer whose voluminous
diatribes evoked no response.

Reforming the realm thus required intensive labours in the
preparation of legislation, the turning of ideas adumbrated in
formal treatises (or private conversation!) into the clauses of a
formal Act of Parliament. I have before this suggested that one
can find such links between the programme of Starkey's *Dialogue*
and some surviving draft acts and enacted drafts.[12] Fortunately
a little evidence survives to display the stages of the process.
Take the document headed:

> That the perfection of such laws which hath been this two
> years thoroughly and indifferently examined by great numbers
> of sage clerks of the realm may not only be published to the
> King's Council and others of good judgment between this and
> next session, but also that all those laws which shall be
> thought expedient for the good of the English Church may
> pass by Act of Parliament.[13]

There are in fact two such lists, but they belong together: handwriting, content, and the double mention of 'between this and
next session' make sure of that. Their date is either November

[10] *Tudor Economic Documents*, ed. R. H. Tawney and E. Power (London,
1924), iii. 121–2.
[11] A. F. Pollard in *Bull.Inst.Hist.Res.* xvi (1938–9), 145–6; but S. T. Bindoff
doubts the connection (*Econ.Hist.Rev.* xiv, 1944, 70).
[12] *Proc. Brit. Acad.* liv (1968), 165ff.
[13] BM. Titus B. i, fos. 159v–60 (*LP* ix. 725).

1534 or October 1535.[14] The second includes apart from legislative proposals a number of administrative memoranda which
leave no doubt that the person who drew them up belonged to
Cromwell's staff. Thus we have here proof that a group of people
connected with him had for two years been compiling a programme of reform embodied in projected statutes. The ones
mentioned are most of them rather drastic and proved too much
for the King's Council. Two of them left a mark on Cromwell's
own notes: the proposal that alien merchants should pay the
same customs duties as natives appears in his memoranda for
October 1534[15] (which is earlier than any date that seems right
for these lists and indicates his participation in the preparatory
stages), and a bill for usury was planned for the spring session
of 1536 though not actually achieved until ten years later.[16] Once
again, we may note the interchange between planners and
minister. However, what matters is the indication of the *modus
operandi*: experts in Cromwell's office laboured over what they
conceived to be the needs of the realm, drafted reforming laws,
got Cromwell to bring them to the attention of King and Council,
and hoped then to see them promoted in Parliament. The distinction between what they proposed and what we know was seriously
undertaken is the distinction between the ideas of the theorists
and what Cromwell regarded as practicable.

Another paper throws further invaluable light on the way in
which these planners worked.[17] As now bound, it looks like a sort
of draft for statutes twenty-two pages long, but this appearance
misleads. It started life as several disparate pieces, though all
written in one hand and occasionally corrected by another (both
unidentified). A few pages and more parts of others are blank;
some pieces of paper have been cut out and off. Certainly, the

---

[14] The later date is indicated by the mention of Sir David Owen's will:
Owen died in Sept. 1535 (*LP* ix. 729[14]). There was no session until that
beginning 4 Feb. 1536, but Parliament had been intended to meet on
3 Nov. 1535 (S. E. Lehmberg, *The Reformation Parliament* [Cambridge,
1970], 217). Since the King is asked to do something by Candlemas
(Feb. 2nd) the seventh session of the Reformation Parliament cannot yet
have been under way. The mention of the present session, however, fits
Oct.–Nov. 1534 much better. The document also mentions that the
proclamation for corn has been drawn: the only one known was dated
11 Nov. 1534 (*TRP* no. 151).

[15] *LP* vi. 1381.   [16] *LP* x. 254; 37 Henry VIII, c. 9.

[17] SP 6/7, art. 14 (*LP* v. 50).

thing is a very long way from being ready for parliamentary purposes. There are signs that parts were copied from earlier drafts; at least one of the suggestions outlined received much fuller working out in yet another draft. The paper thus represents an intermediate stage, collecting proposals for further development. The first nine proposals are explicitly grouped in three 'articles' (that is, three intended statutes), while the remaining eleven form a medley. This comprehensive mixed bag of legislation looks very much like a summary of what 'sage clerks of the realm' had been working on for whatever length of time one may guess, especially as the contents are mixed not only as to targets and purpose but also with respect to the basic attitudes displayed.

The first 'article' is a draft act, preamble and all, for the appointment of a commission to study the alleged demand for an English Bible; this commission, turned into a 'great standing council' for the control of heresy (superseding the bishops' investigatory functions but without powers to prosecute), is also to revise the law of the Church and eliminate from it a 'partiality' for the clergy. The Church courts are further attacked in a clause which bars them from entertaining pleas concerning dilapidations and gives the successor to a parson who has allowed the fabric to decay an action at common law against the executors. The second 'article' runs on without preamble; its two provisions enjoin upon the parish clergy a vigorous observation of traditional practices (a monthly *dirige* and requiem mass, plus prayers for the King, for founders, and for 'all Christian souls'), as well as that burial services and masses for the dead shall be said without fees. The third tackles a mixture of matters touching the Church: there shall be no more grants in mortmain (the King excepted), all beneficed clergy shall give to charity as instructed by two men of the parish (a minimum of 5% of their income), no one shall be barred from holy communion, the Church courts are not to decree anything that might affect lay property contrary to the King's laws, the party grieved to have an injunction out of Chancery, with attachment and treble damages. After a blank page there follow eight points all designed to moderate lay grievances against the clergy. For an 'increase of love, amity and good agreement between the spiritualty and temporalty', both are ordered to stop abusing each other, while priests are not to form 'conspiracies' (combinations designed to defeat the law). Centres of pilgrimage are to arrange for two sermons a year in which the proper meaning of the practice is explained. Such centres are not to increase their takings by spreading their relics over several altars. Talk of alleged miracles is prohibited until the matter has been investigated and approved by the ecclesiastical authorities. Persons likely to profit from pilgrimages are not to impose them (presumably by way of penance) on anyone. The practice of committing children to the life religious is deplored in a preamble and prohibited in an enactment. Lastly, the clergy are forbidden to speak against certain Acts of Parliament: that touching tithe on timber called 'silva cedua' (45 Edward III, c.3), the three reforming acts of 1529, 'ne any statute made in this Parliament'.

This part of the document ends with a list of five points 'to remember': 'doles to be sent home to the people', 'corpus presents', 'priests coming to burials and months' minds', 'that every curate may [damaged] children', 'that no curate shall say that he is not bound to offer the sacrament of the altar ne extreme unction but he be required'. Evidently, no one had yet got round even to a start on drafting legislation for these abuses. There then follows another blank page, and the next separate part switches right away from the subject matter of the first sections. It is an outline proposal for an act against vagabonds: unemployment is to be cured by providing public works on highways 'as shall be thought most expedient by the said council', vagabonds are to appear upon proclamation of such works and to receive reasonable wages, the special 'council' (which is not described in the draft) can make regulations for the work, the King has offered £3000 towards poor relief and promised to turn over the profits from penal statutes, the collection of voluntary alms in common poor chests is to be organized by the council, departure from the works is to be felony, the scheme is to be financed by a comprehensive levy. The remainder of the document, unhappily, is pretty well illegible: it deals in some way with cloth manufacture, the decay of husbandry, and possibly other similar problems.

So what have we here? Three particular proposals for bills touching matters spiritual and the clergy; a second list putting forward possible clauses for acts limiting abuses in the Church; and a third piece offering a series of socio-economic reforms in legislative shape. The last part contains the essential points

which were to be worked up into the remarkable poor-law proposals introduced into Parliament in 1536 (though the notion of
using the yield of penal statutes for poor relief was by then
abandoned!);[18] the other now illegible paragraphs may well have
resulted in other known legislation. Of the first two parts nothing
found its way on to the statute book, but they look very likely to
have been the legislation for the betterment of the Church which,
as we have seen, was urged upon Cromwell's attention in the
heading of the lists discussed before. They also powerfully recall
a general line of anticlerical propaganda usually associated with
the name of Christopher St German. The point about avoiding
mutual abuse is made in St German's *Division between the
Spiritualty and the Temporalty*,[19] while some of the attacks on
the spiritual jurisdiction echo points in the anonymous *Treatise
concerning the Power of the Clergy and the Laws of the Realm*,
also ascribed to St German.[20] That book also complains of the
way in which the law of the Church favours the clergy, wishes to
bar the Church courts from touching lay property, and makes a
special thing of the clergy's attack on the statute *silva cedua*. But
it would be rash to conclude from these echoes that the draft
emerged from St German or reflects his often alleged influence
(never proven) on the Cromwellian reform programme. Quite
apart from the fact that I am not altogether happy about the
ascription of the treatise to St German,[21] the discrepancies be-

[18] Below, pp. 123–4.
[19] Reprinted as an appendix to A. I. Taft's edition of *The Apologye of Syr
Thomas More, Knyght* (London, E.E.T.S., 1930).
[20] *STC* 21588; CUL, Syn . 8 . 53 . 51.
[21] The identification, firmly accepted by F. L. Baumer, 'Christopher St
German: the political philosophy of a Tudor lawyer,' *Amer. Hist. Rev.* 42
(1937), 631–51, rests on an entry in John Bale's catalogue of a work
described as *De cleri potestate ex iure* (Taft, *Apologye*, 259–60). This is
not a very accurate translation of the title of our treatise. More important,
unlike Baumer I cannot see that the pamphlet is like St German's known
work. In the books safely ascribed to him, St German practically never
cites Scripture, while this treatise starts with three chapters which are
nothing but a collection of biblical texts. Certainly the treatise shows
plenty of legal expertise, but there were after all other articulate lawyers
around. It *may* have come from the Cromwell circle proper. – I should
like just to append another small matter. In *Policy and Police*, 173 n.2, I
accepted the opinion, defended by Taft and Pierre Janelle, that there
was a striking resemblance between St German's tract on *Division* and the
Commons' Supplication of 1532. On closer inspection this evaporates.
Taft identified three passages to prove his point, a small enough number
to build a view of St German's alleged influence on the Supplication (on

tween draft and treatise are at least as remarkable as the few coincidences. This is not the place to analyse the whole of that interesting pamphlet; it will suffice to look at the five summing-up points in chapter 19 of which only one, the matter of *silva cedua*, appears in the draft. The much weightier matters in the other four find no reflection: clerical resistance to trial in lay courts, the evasion of the principle by permitting bishops to degrade criminous clerks (a practice the author regards as contrary to the nature of ordination), the clergy's refusal to learn the laws of the realm, their objection to laymen studying canon law. There are other points throughout the book of great importance to its author of which we find nothing in the draft, even though they bore directly on the central issue of the independence of the spiritual jurisdiction. On the other hand, the treatise has nothing on two highly relevant proposals in the draft – the point about dilapidations and the prohibition of grants in mortmain. Lastly, when it comes to the clergy's protests against invasions of their liberty by Acts of Parliament, the treatise speaks only of *silva cedua*, whereas the draft adds the legislation of the Reformation Parliament, immediately a much more obvious point. At most one may suppose – and I think it likely – that the drafting committee had read St German.

There are, in any case, echoes of the draft in more specifically Cromwellian places. The poor law proposals form the outstanding link, but the prohibition of burial fees may connect with an obscurely described bill for 'portions in lieu of mortuaries' introduced but not passed in the 1532 session,[22] and the concern for an English Bible is assuredly better vouched for in the group that gathered round Cromwell than in anything written by St German. So is the inclination to solve the problems of the day by creating new administrative bodies – 'councils'. The arguments about proper ceremonies, the partiality of the clerical jurisdiction, and the issue of dilapidations recur in a note from Cromwell's staff in

which alone Janelle rested his argument that St German was officially retained). But even these three will not serve. (1) Taft, 335 (and 153, l. 5): there is no similarity at all between the two passages cited. (2) Taft, 339 (and 165, l. 24): comparison between the two passages reveals no verbal and only the most superficial substantive resemblance. (3) Taft, 341 (and 171, l. 33): St German's whole point is the power of bodily arrest of which there is not one word in the Supplication.

[22] *LP* vi. 120(1).

1536.[23] St German can, however, contribute to the dating of the draft, if we accept that his books were out before it was put together. His pamphlet on the clergy's power (if it was his) should probably be dated 1533, while the one on *Division* belongs unquestionably to 1532; and circa 1534, rather than the calendar's dating of 1529, fits the contents of the composite draft.[24] A later date is ruled out by the very traditional attitude towards prayers for the dead and ceremonies in general. This attitude – to reform some abuses which exploit the people's credulity but not to abate a jot of the principles from which the abuses sprang – also makes it unlikely that only one mind stood behind this diverse collection of proposals. The case I made before for assigning the poor-law draft to William Marshall seems to me still convincing, and Marshall was throughout a radical in matters of religion.[25]

In any case, the appearance of the document makes its origins plain: it is a redaction of several separate proposals, put together as a programme of reforms in Church and commonwealth but intended to be separated out again for full-scale drafting. That evidently was the way things were done. Ideas concerning needed reforms were current among the writers and planners; rough outlines or brief notes on steps to be taken were then jotted down, as for instance in the list of 'things necessary, as it seemeth, to be remembered before the breaking up of the Parliament' drawn up in late 1534;[26] on occasion these could be assembled in more worked up form, as in our draft; and lastly particular bills might be drawn for the Parliament, like the poor-law bill of 1536 and possibly the draft for a bill proposing a standing commission to

---

23 SP 1/99, fos. 227–8 (*LP* ix. 1065). The date is fixed by the mention of the King's acquisition of first fruits, tenths and suppressed lands.

24 Since the reforming acts of 1529 are mentioned, 1530 would be the earliest date; since unspecified other anticlerical legislation is also referred to, the sessions of 1532 and 1533 (Acts of Annates and Appeals) are likely to have been past, too.

25 Cf. *Econ. Hist. Rev.* 2nd series, vi (1953), 65–6.

26 BM, Cleo. E. vi, fo. 330 (*LP* vii. 1383), and SP 1/105, fo. 56 (*LP* xi. 83), two papers which quite obviously belong together since they have the same heading and deal in part with the same matters. I prefer the 1534 dating to 1536 because it fits the situation much better. The list resembles the composite draft in mentioning problems of the relations between spirituality and temporalty as well as commonwealth matters, and it also mentions *silva cedua*, but it firmly comes out against prayers for the dead and the worship of images.

assist bishops in heresy cases, though that sets up a rather different body from that envisaged by the composite draft.[27] So far as we know, most of the proposals worked out in this list did not progress further, but our knowledge is limited, nor does the fact reduce the value of the document in explaining how Cromwellian planning worked. One thing that emerges from all this discussion is that planning is the right word: ideas that ultimately appeared on the statute book can be traced in development for several years before.

Thus one might suppose that by taking the notes and proposals for reform plus the statute book one might establish what Cromwell's administration was trying to do and how far it succeeded, and in so far as any attempt to assess its work has yet been made that has been the method. Unfortunately, the story is a great deal less simple than that. In the first place, humanist reformers, or for that matter Thomas Cromwell and his planning staff, were far from being the only people to recognize the significance of parliamentary legislation. And in the second, the statute book poses some extremely difficult problems concerning initiative and influence.

A meeting of Parliament acted as a signal to all the interests in the realm – especially those one may call organized – to prepare their grievances for an airing, and in practice they usually did this by drafting legislation which they wanted to see passed. The most formidable lobby of all was the city of London which had developed a smooth routine for getting its bills prepared and into Parliament and which, though often unsuccessful, never ceased to work for its own ends.[28] The second city was not far behind. In February 1532 the city council of York resolved to promote four bills in Parliament and sent George Gayle, alderman, and Miles Newton, city clerk, to London to organize the move. Pressure was applied in letters for support to Cromwell (who received a small gift) and Audley (who received only prayers); Sir George Lawson, a Cromwell client and one of York's representatives in the Commons, was instructed to assist in the appeal to Cromwell, and the recorder, apparently in London on

---

[27] SP 1/151, fos. 132–9 (*LP* xiv. I. 876: *LP*'s 1539 date is purely conjectural).

[28] Helen Miller, 'London and Parliament in the Reign of Henry VIII,' *Bull. Inst. Hist. Res.* xxxv (1962), 128–49.

his own business, was told to approach both ministers.[29] All four
measures would have been beneficial to the city but offended
other interests; only one of them, prohibiting fish-garths in the
Ouse and Humber, became law.[30] A year later the council revived
one of the failed bills, namely that waste space created in city
and suburbs by the pulling down of houses should be converted
to common use; they also hoped to secure the repeal, 'if it be
possible', of the recent Act for Sewers 'forasmuch as it is not
beneficial to York'.[31] Continued failure proved discouraging; in
May 1536, the council, perhaps taken by surprise when the dissolution of the Reformation Parliament was followed so quickly
by the calling of another, had no instructions for the city members
touching bills in Parliament, but asked them to act as general
agents in private suits to Cromwell and Audley.[32] However, after
the Pilgrimage of Grace Cromwell got more directly involved in
Yorkshire affairs, with agents of his inspecting the local problems,
and York felt encouraged to try for another reform. In March
1540 Richard Layton was persuaded to suggest to Cromwell that
in the forthcoming session of Parliament something might be
done about the excessive number of malt kilns in York: they had
led to economic decline in the city and were causing 'all the
town to be ale-tipplers'. This approach was followed up by John
Uvedale, clerk of the Council in the North and another Cromwell
client, who forwarded a bill on the subject (cast in the form of a
petition to the King requesting the enactment of a statute) which
he asked the minister to revise and promote.[33] But York was un-
lucky, or too far away: once again nothing was done, though a
bill for cloth-making in York, of which we know nothing else, got
a first reading in the Lords.[34]

Great towns were not the only interests aware of the possibilities of Parliament. In 1539, the weavers of Suffolk and Essex
organized a protest against the 1536 Act for the better manufacture of cloth which was very unpopular with the producers
because it was intended to safeguard the interests of the con-

---

[29] *York Civic Records*, ed. A. Raine (Yorks. Archaeol. Soc.), iii (1942), 138–
141.   [30] 23 Henry VIII, c. 18.
[31] *York Civic Records*, iii. 146.   [32] Ibid. iv. 3–4.
[33] Ellis, iii. III. 211–13; SP 1/159, fos. 84–5; 243, fos. 41–2 (*LP* v. 515;
    Add. 1453). The bill claimed that the multitude of maltsters had destroyed
    both the balance of employment at York and all timber for thirty miles
    around.   [34] *LJ* i. 130b.

sumers.[35] Earlier protests had obtained a one-year suspension of
the act by proclamation, a reluctant concession to the plea that
the act forced weavers to acquire new equipment which they had
not yet had time to buy, but this expired on 29 September 1538.[36]
Thus in 1539 the weaving interests promoted a repealing act
which, however, stuck in the Commons; they therefore appealed
to Cromwell for aid, to all appearance in vain.[37] The kersey-
makers tried another approach. They petitioned the Council,
asking that both Houses of Parliament be requested to debate the
1536 act, with a view to determining whether it was 'for the
advancement of the commonwealth of his realm'; no action
resulted.[38] The London fishmongers did a little better in 1536.
They promoted a bill designed to protect their interest against
purveyors to royal and noble households who were selling surplus
fish below market price; this passed the Commons but died in the
Lords.[39] It is hard to say who was behind a bill to exempt certain
schoolmasters from the payment of first fruits and tenths.[40] The
draft, which is all we have, has an official appearance, and there
are references to foundations 'for the erudition, instruction and
virtuous bringing up of youth in civil manners and good letters'
as well as to 'the continuance of a public or a common wealth'
which echo the language of the government-connected reformers.
On the other hand, the generalizations of the preamble are tied to
the single example of the schoolmaster of St Mary Wick in Cornwall. It is quite possible that that individual thought to serve his
own interests best by calling for a general concession. It is no
easier to know what to make of an appeal to Lords and Commons
from the poor and impotent people forced to beg and starve by
the delinquencies of masters of hospitals: what sort of organization could possibly have claimed to speak for such a body? An
eighteenth-century endorsement says that the petition was presented in the Parliament of 4 Henry VIII (1513), on what grounds
it is impossible to say; but since the bill asked for the intervention
of founders' heirs, and since the founders' heirs of the hospital of

[35] 27 Henry VIII, c. 12.   [36] *TRP* i. 258–9.   [37] *LP* xiv. I. 874.
[38] St Ch 2/23/115. It appears from this petition that a second proclamation,
    now lost, may have continued the suspension till 24 June 1539.
[39] SP 1/239, fos. 278–81 (*LP Add.* 1049); *LJ* i. 67b.
[40] SP 1/104, fos. 151–4 (*LP* x. 1092). The suggested date (1536) is based on
    the fact that in the Parliament of 28 Henry VIII the Universities did
    obtain exemption.

Sherburn near Durham tried in the Parliament of 1536 for an act in their own favour, the general petition may belong to a concerted effort of that date.[41]

The problem, of course, is to know what lay behind moves less readily assignable to this or that interest. Take the case of Dover harbour. In 1539, an act was drafting for the repair and restoration of the pier there; all that survives is the preamble, very long, full of explanations about the needs of defence and so forth, and heavily corrected by Cromwell.[42] Is this draft to be linked with the petition from the town for the repair of the harbour?[43] That is to say, was Cromwell using an undoubted private petition to promote a reform of his own, or was he helping a private interest to gain its ends, or were the two things unconnected? It is not always possible to conclude official origin from the appearance of Cromwell's hand on a draft. Thus his assistance to the city of Salisbury, which wanted an act to improve the quality of the bishop's bailiff, belongs almost certainly to his private practice.[44] The act of 23 Henry VIII, c.8, for tin works and harbours in Devon and Cornwall, was effectively drafted by him, but its phrasing can leave little doubt that it was promoted by the locality.[45] An act thus passed in 1532 could well have been in hand for a little time, and this may again have been a sample of private practice. But what of the Pewterers' Act of 1534 (25 Henry VIII, c. 9) for which we also have a draft much corrected by Cromwell?[46] From its phrasing and general import this must also have been a private bill, yet by this late date it is not credible that Cromwell, busy enough in all conscience on major parliamentary matters, should still have been available as parliamentary counsel to a very sectional interest. The draft as corrected

---

[41] The general petition is E 175/65; that for Sherburn is SP 1/96, fos. 206–7 (*LP* ix. 401[2]). *LP* hide the full impact of the second by omitting the last demand, namely that founders' heirs should be empowered to resume all gifts to the hospital at their discretion.

[42] SP 2/P, fos. 128–32. The dating in *LP* vii. 66(2) is wrong: the details recited about rebuilding forts etc. put this document into 1539 at the earliest.

[43] *L.P.* vii 66(10). No reliable date can be assigned to this document.

[44] Cf. *Policy and Police*, 101.

[45] The draft is SP 2/L, fos. 106–11 (*LP* v. 722[8]); Cromwell's plentiful corrections appear in the act as passed. All this renders mysterious a note of Cromwell's early in 1536 touching an act for the same purpose (*LP* x. 254): perhaps some amendment was contemplated.

[46] SP 2/P. fo. 23 (*LP* vii. 62).

still differs markedly from the eventual act, so that it may belong to an attempt made in an earlier session of Parliament, a conjecture (which would again place the business safely into private practice) supported by the fact that the draft was among Cromwell's papers before the end of 1532.[47]

Thus even where Cromwell appears we should not automatically speak of government initiative. Yet we need to decide such problems of legislative initiative at every turn. Parliamentary legislation was not the monopoly of either government or of dedicated reformers connected with government, and it cannot be taken for granted that bills 'for the common weal', especially economic legislation, originated with Cromwell or his men. Nothing, in fact, could be further from the truth than A. F. Pollard's confident assertion, widely believed ever since, that after 1461 the 'new monarchy' dominated legislative activity until in the reign of Elizabeth private members are found promoting public bills.[48] Private members were doing just that throughout the fifteenth and sixteenth centuries, and if we are to discover what the reform movement under Cromwell attempted and achieved we must endeavour to distinguish between bills officially promoted and those originating with a private interest.

The evidence of pre-parliamentary activity, patchy as it is, leaves too many problems unsolved; can we get any help from the evidence of what happened in Parliament? Here again we are ill-served both by the sources and by what has been said about them. Legislative procedure in the reign of Henry VIII remains obscure and often bewildering, and I cannot on this occasion treat the subject at length.[49] Still, something must be said about it, especially about some of the hampering errors that have been propagated. The two worst, both sanctified by Pollard, are that in the Reformation Parliament bills were nearly always introduced in the Commons (for tactical reasons), and that bills were introduced on paper, only so-called bills of grace (signed by the King) being at once presented on parchment.[50] The first allegation is

---

[47] *LP* vi. 299(ix).   [48] In *Eng. Hist. Rev.* lvii (1942), 225.

[49] A study of legislative procedure in the years 1536–47 is being undertaken by Mr J. I. Miklovich; I write subject to his later correction.

[50] *Eng. Hist. Rev.* lvii (1942), 49. Lehmberg, *Reformation Parliament*, avoids the discussion of procedure – perhaps wisely. However, in consequence he also avoids the discussion of initiative. I shall have to go over some of the ground covered by him from a different point of view.

readily disproved by even the most casual glance at the Original Acts in the House of Lords which always show in which House a bill originated; the second by a more intensive study of those acts, all on parchment, which shows them to be written in a great variety of hands and style, frequently unofficial by any standard; this puts it right out of the question that they could be the product of regular engrossing (transcription onto parchment) in either House. Some bills were certainly introduced on paper, but the very fact that the Journal of the House of Lords occasionally notes the point strongly suggests that it was not the invariable rule.[51] This 'immature' practice explains such difficulties as the instructions to Cromwell in 1531 that the bills for treasons, for sewers and for apparel be got ready and engrossed 'against the beginning of the next Parliament',[52] or his own note in 1534 that he had to see to the engrossing of two bills for the forthcoming session.[53] Evidently, therefore, at least some of the extant Original Acts are the very documents which were at the start introduced into Parliament, which means that sometimes they can tell us more about the origin and fate of bills than a parliamentary engrossment would; while on the other hand difficulties now exist, with consequences for interpretation, in deciding at what stage the surviving document was produced. As for Pollard's 'acts of grace' signed by the King, the royal signature is curiously haphazard in our period. Little sense can at present be made of the pattern, and variations are great between one Parliament and another. I cannot sort those problems now, but it will be apparent that reliance on procedure as described a hundred, or even fifty, years later can seriously mislead.

We must, in fact, approach the parliamentary materials with an open mind, ready to learn what they may tell, but stoically prepared to be sadly disappointed. What we have is of three kinds. The Rolls of Parliament, entirely formal, tell very little of interest. We possess a Lords' Journal for four out of the nine sessions (1531–1540) with which we are concerned, and the evidence it provides throws so much light that one is led to be very cautious about judging the events of the other five sessions

[51] I fully agree with the opinion of S. E. Lehmberg, 'Early Tudor Parliamentary Procedures,' *Eng. Hist. Rev.* lxxxv (1970), 1–11, esp. 2–3.
[52] *StP* i. 381–2. A parchment form of the 1532 treason bill, never introduced in Parliament, survived among Cromwell's papers (*Policy and Police*, 272).
[53] *LP* vii. 49.

in the absence of such evidence. Some proposals, for instance, found in draft or note form are known to have reached Parliament in the sessions covered by the Journal; very likely, therefore, more of this puzzling material could be assigned if we had more Journals. At times the Journals tell us of the drafting of acts in the House itself, a warning against necessarily supposing that what seems like government business was always introduced prepared. But the Journals also create problems. They certainly do not contain a complete account of the Lords' business: thus in 1536 two acts indubitably passed receive no mention at all. The record of readings is often incomplete. The Journals sometimes suggest a different House of origin from that vouched for by the Original Act; this can be an important clue to events in Parliament. The total absence of a Commons' Journal, which did not start until 1547, is, of course, a most serious matter. Our most systematic evidence, in fact, are the Original Acts, preserved virtually complete for the nine sessions in question.[54] They tell us about the House of origin, and such amendments as appear on attached schedules can also be assigned. Since bills may so frequently have been introduced on parchment, it is not possible to say (as one can say for later Parliaments) that amendments on the face of the document itself were always made at a late stage in the first House to consider it; but they are in any case very few, and something can occasionally be made of them. I have found two endorsements of committees, no more; this proves that bills were sometimes committed (and committed in parchment form!), but not that only those two were.

The first question to which these materials should provide an answer touches the distinction between public and private acts, one of the more enduring problems of parliamentary historians. It is at least a sensible assumption that acts forming part of a government programme of reform would be public; if we could distinguish, we could eliminate a whole group of acts. We have two criteria by which to judge the distinction – the distinction, I repeat, between public and private acts, not that between public and private bills which may be even more significant but seems to have left no evidence at all for this period. In the first place,

---

[54] A few acts are lost. None survives for the first session of the Reformation Parliament, but since the work of that session cannot be treated as part of Cromwell's reforms that does not matter here.

the royal assent was supposed to be given in different forms: *le roi le veult* for public acts, and *soit fait comme il est desiré* for private. But for three sessions (27, 28 and 31 Henry VIII) the formula of assent was, most improperly, not inscribed on the act, for reasons which may be conjectured, no more;[55] and though the roll records assents, we have reason to think that it could differ from the act on occasion, no one at present being sure which is to be believed. In any case, it would seem that the real grounds on which the assent was varied touched neither the contents of the bill nor the source from which it came, but only the formula of introduction. Bills adopting a petitionary form are generally assented to *soit fait*, those cast in the form of a resolution by King and Parliament are replied to *le roi le veult*. This means, in the first place, that despite the textbooks the distinction by formula of assent does not in fact coincide with such divisions between public and private acts as, according to other evidence, the age was making; and secondly, it is not a useful distinction to us because perfectly official bills at times, for reasons of policy, adopted the petitionary form and thus received the private assent. Many attainders, for instance, are petitions and therefore 'private acts', though no one will suppose that the government was not behind the bills attacking the Nun of Kent, the Poles and Courtenays, or Thomas Cromwell. The First Succession Act, manifestly and provably a government measure, is a petition, and so are the Dispensations Act and the first Act for the Dissolution of the Monasteries – and the first two of these three (for which alone the formula of assent exists) were assented to *soit fait*. That makes at least two, possibly three, of the outstanding government measures of the decade into 'private acts'.

The other and more real distinction between public and private

[55] The session of 28 Henry VIII ended with the chancellor announcing the King's approval of bills passed, but no formal assent was given before the dissolution; that of 31 Henry VIII was prorogued after a similar statement from the chancellor. We have no Journal for 27 Henry VIII, the last session of the Reformation Parliament. In 1540, on the other hand, when the assent was marked on the acts, the fact of it is expressly mentioned in the Journal (*LJ* i. 101, 125, 162). Thus possibly in this reign the bills of some sessions, in the King's absence, received only a general approval to be turned later into the formal assent noted on the roll which, of course, was required to turn bill into act; but who then decided which formula should be enrolled? There is evidence that the clerk of the Crown in Chancery adjusted various formulae on the Roll, to suit his routine; but this requires fuller discussion on another occasion.

acts took note of this technicality and included some such *soit fait* acts in the public section. The test is enrolment and publication. At a later date, the King's printer was supposed to produce the full text of the public acts and merely a list of the private, and the criterion apparently applied was the distinction between acts that would have to pay fees (private) and those that did not. In the reign of Henry VIII, the situation is less clear. Down to 28 Henry VIII (1536) all acts were enrolled, without visible distinction; yet the King's printer included only 'general' (public?) acts in the statute of the year. He adopted the order still followed in the chapter numbering of the statute book, whereas the roll usually started with matters touching the King's private estate, followed by private acts touching subjects' affairs, with the general acts last, sometimes in an order different from the printer's.[56] In 1539, the clerk of the Parliaments for the first time, officially, on the roll, divided the production of the session into fourteen public and fourteen private acts, but all twenty-eight were enrolled. In the next session, the roll did not again record this careful division, but for the first time a large number of private acts (and indeed, for assignable reasons, two general acts) failed to get enrolled.[57] Also from 1539, general (public) acts came first on the roll, in the order also adopted by the printer, followed by such private acts as were enrolled. This might almost suggest that the whole business of enrolment fees for private acts was introduced in 1539 when Thomas Soulemont, lately private secretary to Cromwell, became deputy clerk of the Parliaments and effective occupant of the office. On the other hand, it does seem as though throughout the 1530's (when sessional printing appears to have taken place) the King's printer printed only those acts which we would consider to be public, because general: since all acts were enrolled, how did he know how to distinguish? As he included some assented to *soit fait* he evidently paid no particular heed to the formula of assent. At this point, until a study of parliamentary printing in these early days has been made, it would be absurd to come to conclusions; even tentative ones are hardly in place.

[56] There is an exception in 1529 when the roll inexplicably reverses the order.

[57] 32 Henry VIII: 80 acts passed. Of the 51 public acts, two (the general pardon and the subsidy) were not enrolled, probably because they were very long and had been separately printed at an earlier stage. Of the 29 private acts, only 11 were enrolled.

All one can say is that the printer, and in due course the clerk, have left evidence that the distinction was understood to exist, and we ought to pay attention to what was chosen for printing if we want to know the contemporary position. The upshot of even a superficial test turns out to be disconcerting: those definable as private because not printed include some attainders, the first (conditional) restraint of annates, and the dissolution of the lesser monasteries – all government measures; those he printed include all statutes later to be defined as 'local' which there is every reason to think were the product of local initiative.[58]

Thus none of the parliamentary materials gives systematic answers to what must be our first question: can we ascribe a given act 'for the commonwealth' to the initiative of the government, of Cromwell, or of that known and identifiable group of reformers who worked for and through him? Every case needs to be treated on its own merits, with a good many remaining in doubt. The only point about which I have become fully convinced is that an act which starts by declaring that the King has considered or remembered a problem and wishes to take action is indeed official; the reverse (e.g. the pretence of a petition) does not apply.

Let me illustrate the difficulties with a few examples. There survives an interesting draft bill of 1536 which proposed to compel the inhabitants of ecclesiastical liberties in all the towns of England to obey the decrees of civic authorities and pay local taxes.[59] The interests served are particular, and the draft, though careful and spaced to allow for corrections, is not in the hand of any one of Cromwell's drafting clerks. For that reason, I originally classified it as an abortive draft from outside the government.[60] However, it is not cast in the form of a petition but uses the formulae of an official measure, and its very long preamble, filling more than two thirds of the whole, also rather hints at an official origin – long preambles were unusual in private enter-

---

[58] This discussion of the printer's practice is based on a highly preliminary study of two contemporary collections of statutes in CUL (Sel . 3 . 207 and Rel . b . 5 . 53). A great deal more work is needed, especially in the collections in BM and the Bodleian Library; the mysteries are many.
[59] SP 6/1, fos. 66–7 (LP xv. 501). The date is given by the entry in LJ; LP mistakenly associated the draft with 32 Henry VIII, c. 12, and therefore opted for 1540.
[60] Bull. Inst. Hist. Res. xxv (1952), 132.

prises. It was introduced in the Lords,[61] where private initiatives of this sort were certainly less likely than in the Commons; exceptions do occur. It received only one reading before vanishing; which does not suggest that the government stood behind it, nor was it introduced by the lord chancellor who, to judge from the Lords' Journal, was in that session responsible for government bills in that House. The draft itself contains a hint that it may have been the culmination of a genuine agitation: the bill complains of counter-propaganda by the persons affected, 'as by some of their letters in this present Parliament shown partly it may appear' – a precious indication of the sophisticated manoeuvres employed in the politics of the day. Taking these few and in part contradictory facts together, I am still inclined to ascribe the bill to private initiative, but it is obviously impossible to be certain.

Activities in Parliament were real enough, as two bills of the first session of 1534 will show. Both were planned by Cromwell. One was to deal with the sale of butter and cheese, and Cromwell personally saw to its engrossment on the eve of the session.[62] It passed the Commons readily enough, but the Lords rejected it, after four readings: we cannot tell why.[63] A bill for improving the breed of horses – a constant preoccupation of a government concerned about military preparedness – never reached the Commons, for the Lords, who saw it first, turned it down on third reading.[64] However, in this matter Cromwell persisted: he resolved to reintroduce the bill in the last session of the Reformation Parliament, using formulae which emphasized the King's personal concern, and this time the Lords accepted it.[65] This sort of thing shows how unwise it would be to assume a simple line from intention to execution or guess an equally straight line from execution to intention.

Even acts that no one has ever doubted emerged from government initiative prove, on closer inspection, to pose surprising problems. The Dispensations Act, passed in the spring session of 1534, ought to be quite straightforward. It is cast in the form of a Commons' petition, requesting action by King and Parliament. The first entry in the Lords' Journal therefore fits the case: on

---

[61] *LJ* i. 95a. [62] *LP* vii. 49.
[63] *LJ* i. 73a, 74a–b. [64] Ibid. 64a, 78a.
[65] *LP* x. 254; 27 Henry VIII, c. 6 (introduced first in the Lords).

March 12th, four bills were brought in from the Commons including one 'for the abrogation of the payment of monies called
Peter's Pence and of the granting of dispensations by the bishop
of Rome'.[66] On the next day, this received a first reading,[67] but
the description twice used in the Journal never reappears. Instead
there is mention on the 14th of a bill transmitted from the Commons 'for the abrogation of the authority [later called usurped
authority] of the bishop of Rome', which received a second
reading and was committed to the lord chancellor.[68] The simplest
and likeliest, explanation is that the bill is the same and that the
clerk found a shorter (though less accurate) title for it; certainly
no other bill suitable for that description passed in that session.
On the 19th the bill was read a third time together with a proviso,
both bill and proviso being once more delivered to the lord
chancellor.[69] On the following day the Lords gave the bill a
fourth reading, passed it, sent it to the Commons by the hands of
the clerk of the Crown, and received it back 'sped' from the
Commons – the correct procedure for a bill initiated in the Lower
House and amended in the Upper.[70] That should have been the
end of it, but ten days later, on the last day of the session, another
proviso was introduced in the Lords, read three times, and sent to
the Commons, where the new addition was also read three times
before being sped and returned for the royal assent.[71]

In the main the Original Act supports both this history and the
identification of this bill with the Dispensations Act. There are
two separate schedules attached to the bill, both initiated in the
Lords and assented to by the Commons, and although each contains more than one proviso (five and two respectively) there are
good grounds for thinking that the Journal would describe any
single piece of parchment adding new clauses as 'una provisio',
no matter how many clauses it contained.[72] However, according
to the annotations on the Original Act, the bill itself (not only the
schedules) was first despatched from the Lords to the Commons
who assented to both bill and proviso. This presupposes an origin

---

[66] *LJ* i. 74b: 'concernens abrogationem solutionis pecuniarum vocatarum
Peter Pence, et concessionis dispensationum num per Romanum ponti-
ficem'.   [67] Ibid. 75a.
[68] Ibid. 75b.   [69] Ibid. 77a.
[70] Ibid. 77b.   [71] Ibid. 81b.
[72] Cf. the Sheep Bill of this session where the schedule of nine provisos is
also called one proviso (ibid. 80a).

in the House of Lords and makes no sense at all. A bill explicitly drawn in the name of the House of Commons cannot have originated in the Lords, and amendment by schedule was the method employed by the second House to see the bill, not the House of origin. Even if it be supposed that the Lords exceptionally amended a bill of their own by means of a schedule of provisos, the Journal, which on every occasion describes the bill as transmitted from the Commons, leaves no doubt that the bill's introductory formula is correct: it originated in the Lower House. There are several available explanations, ranging from the possibility that the change of title in the Journal in fact represents the appearance of a totally different bill which failed to pass (highly improbable) to the most likely: namely that during the five days when Lord Chancellor Audley had the bill a new copy was made for some reason to which the Lords' amendments were attached, and that the clerk of the Parliaments slipped by inscribing a delivery instruction on this unannotated copy which was strictly misleading. One may suppose the existence of an original bill, now lost, which had been correctly despatched from Commons to Lords.[73] Not that this really solves all the problems or actually explains what happened; the inwardness of this reconstruction needs more attention than can be given to it here.

One thing, however, emerges from this confusion. If the Dispensations Act was official, or at least Cromwellian (and its whole tenor shows that it was), its committal for revision to Lord Chancellor Audley together with that very belated afterthought which suddenly suspended the effect of the act till the King should have confirmed it by letters patent indicates discordant counsels within the government itself. Did Henry know what was going forward? The mess into which this very important bill got suggests strongly that Cromwell, in the Commons, was moving faster than the King found himself able to follow, an interpretation supported by the note for some very drastic anti-papal legislation planned on the eve of the session but of which nothing materialized.[74]

That conventional notions of these interrelationships of King,

---

[73] The Dispensations Act, long though it was, was copied at speed for the letters patent, dated a week after the end of the session, which brought it into effect (*Statutes of the Realm,* iii. 471).
[74] BM, Titus B. i, fo. 161 (*LP* vi. 1381 [3]).

minister and Parliament may well be too simple is also suggested
by another act of this session: the important measure limiting the
number of sheep an individual might own.[75] On the face of it,
this is plainly a product of 'commonwealth' thinking. Its form is
official enough, and the preamble makes all the right noises about
wicked profiteers. The act tried to deal with the most familiar
grievance of the day and one of the reformers' standard complaints: More, Starkey and Armstrong, for instance, were all
agreed about the evils of this 'capitalist' sheep-farming. It tried
an original remedy: instead of the usual injunction to destroy
enclosures and restore land to husbandry it limited individual
holdings of sheep to 2000. The impression that we have here a
striking product of Cromwellian reform is supported by a letter
from Cromwell to the King (undated, unfortunately) in which he
informs Henry that 'yesterday there passed your Commons' a bill
restricting owners of sheep to 2000 animals and compelling every
man 'being a farmer' to keep one eighth of his land permanently
under tillage. Cromwell hoped the King would assist the passage
of this bill 'amongst your Lords above', by which help he would
'do the most noble, profitable and most beneficial thing that ever
was done for the common wealth of this your realm' – the best
thing done since Brutus' time.[76] So far a perfectly straightforward
case, except that one may be surprised at Henry's ignorance of
what was going on in the Lower House and his unawareness of
his minister's socio-economic measures. There is, however, an
immediate note of warning in the fact that the act as passed
shows no trace of the second provision mentioned by Cromwell.

The whole story falls apart the moment one looks at the
Original Act and the Lords' Journal. The bill now extant was
introduced in the Lords, not the Commons, and it includes the
essential provision concerning the number of sheep, a few harm-
less qualifying clauses, and a proviso limiting actions under the
statute to within one year after the offence.[77] In this form it was
sent to the Commons who, exceptionally, committed it. The
labours of the committee produced a sheet of amendments by

[75] 25 Henry VIII, c. 13. The substance of the act is discussed below, pp.
101–6.
[76] Merriman, i. 373. Cromwell fulsomely excused his effrontery in suggesting a course of action to the King by stressing the duty and love he owed
to his majesty and the common wealth of the realm.
[77] Sections 1–6.

way of provisos which is as large as the original bill – nine of them altogether. The Lords agreed to them but added a further proviso. All these moves came towards the end of the session: the first mention in the Journal occurs on March 26th when the clerk noted that the bill had been brought in from the Commons with a proviso. On the 27th the House read the bill and proviso a third time, or possibly three times. On the 28th, the bill, now mysteriously called one transmitted from the Commons (i.e. originally theirs), was given to Sir Anthony Fitzherbert to consider – a suitable choice since the learned judge was also an expert on husbandry. On the 30th it came back before the House, rather strangely received another third reading, and after assent was sent down to the Commons (for their assent to the last proviso) from whence it returned safely the same day. It was then sped in readiness for the royal assent.[78]

The Journal and Original Bill make it plain that this was a Lords' bill which the Commons qualified severely by their amendments. Yet Cromwell thought of it as a Commons' bill which needed royal assistance to pass the Lords, and he treated it as a product of his own proper zeal for the common weal. The record cannot lie; Cromwell cannot have been so totally mistaken. I suggest that the way out of this conflict of testimony may be found in the two small pieces of evidence which do not quite fit their respective sides of the story: Cromwell's description of the bill which adds an enactment not found in the act as passed, and the clerk's description of it at a late stage as transmitted from below when in fact it had originated in the Lords. It would thus appear that there was an original Commons' bill, got through early in the session, which immediately ran into hot water in the Lords, a development which gave time for more general opposition to so drastic a measure to gather itself together. The urgency of Cromwell's appeal to the King, quite uncommonly anxious, flamboyant and deferential, lends support to the notion that he realized he had got it past the Commons before opposition there managed to rally and wanted no delay upstairs. In this he failed, and it must be conjectured that the Lords replaced the Commons' bill with a new one (a fairly common practice at the time). The fact that the Journal remains silent until after the substituted bill had come back from the Commons reflects on the clerk, not on

78 *LJ* i. 80a–b, 81a–b.

this reconstruction. The government succeeded in keeping one main purpose of the bill but lost some points in it; they also had, presumably, to accept some limiting provisoes not in the original bill. Worse still, the task of persuading the Commons was to do again, and this time opposition had been forewarned. The upshot was still quite a good and useful bill, but one markedly less drastic than Cromwell and the commonwealth men had wanted. The story tells a good deal about the realities of pushing a reform programme through what in England was the only instrument available for achieving major change.

A great many people besides the government wished to use Parliament for their purposes; the government themselves did not always form a solid entity with coherent plans; the surviving evidence too often prevents us from linking plans and new laws to the initiative of those reformers who, we know, gravitated to Cromwell in the hope of seeing their ideas realized in his administration. However, there is no need to despair totally. In the eight years of Cromwell's ascendancy a great many new laws were made for the commonwealth, and of that number a good part can be securely linked with him and his men. The evidence of drafts and acts is sometimes ambiguous, but it does not always deprive us of the knowledge we seek. In addition we have the very considerable help of Cromwell's notes and other papers from his office in which the preparation of legislation occurs frequently. That from the first he made himself the Council's expert on parliamentary affairs is certain enough. It looks as though he took control in 1531, in the second session of the Reformation Parliament. By the middle of that year it was reported from London that this unknown councillor was doing as he pleased in Parliament;[79] and when the session ended he gathered up the unfinished bills, to the sizable number of twenty-nine, and deposited them in his counting-house.[80] Some of these bills, as we shall see, he continued to promote on later occasions. In September that year he received Henry's personal instructions for, among other things, the preparation of bills, work to be done in cooperation with the King's legal counsel who normally drafted government

[79] *LP* v. 628.
[80] SP 1/56, fos. 14r–v (*LP* iv. 6043[3]). The list makes better sense for 1531 than for the *LP* dating of 1529, which is not to say that some bills may not have been hanging since the first session.

legislation.[81] At the end of the next session, in May 1532, he again took charge of bills unfinished in the Commons of which this time there were sixteen, six having been read twice and the remainder only once.[82] There are at this time notes of bills filed among his office papers which do not match with these unfinished bills and represent proposals worked out but not yet used.[83] Thereafter his 'remembrances' – memoranda of things to be done or to be discussed with Henry – frequently mention prospective legislation. These materials provide a list of legislative proposals with which Cromwell can definitely be associated, and together with what the less indisputable evidence can safely yield this list forms a firm basis for analysing the intentions and achievements of this reforming minister and his planning staff.

Not that the better known members of that staff, who all joined after the beginning of 1535, can claim a share in the work of the early days. The chronology of reform is of some interest. Cromwell entered Parliament in November 1529, hoping there to make himself 'better regarded'. He was already something of an old hand, having sat in 1523; since the last Parliament before that had met in 1515 there can have been hardly anyone with greater experience than his. But in 1529 he was only a private member, and though he certainly sat on the committee for the bill attacking royal letters of protection which was promoted by London, and though he pretty certainly played his part in the anticlerical moves of the session, it is not possible to ascribe its legislation to him.[84] In any case, there were but six acts for the common weal passed that year, none of them novel or major. In 1531, Cromwell had achieved much greater prominence and was a councillor, but he was still a long way from running an administration dominated by the duke of Norfolk in politics and the lord chancellor, Sir Thomas More, in matters of law, a fact which may have been partly responsible for the Lords' activity that session:

---

[81] *StP* i. 381–2. [82] *LP* vi. 120(1).
[83] Ibid. 299(ix).
[84] 'Protections' were exceptions from legal action at private suit obtained by people going abroad and wishing to escape hostile moves made in their absence. For the bill cf. Miller, *Bull. Inst. Hist. Res.* xxxv (1962), 144. The unsuccessful bill (*LP Add.* 663) remained in Cromwell's archive (*LP* vi. 299[ix]). It is likely also that in this first session he took charge of the agitation which ultimately produced the Supplication against the Ordinaries (my remarks in *Eng. Hist. Rev.* lxvi [1951], 507–34).

four out of seven reform acts started in the Upper House.[85] By
early 1532, on the other hand, he was well forward on the Council
and, as we have seen, expressly made responsible for government
legislation; it can hardly be a coincidence that from that session
onwards reform bills come thick and fast and at first almost
always start in the Commons. In 1532, despite the time spent on
the Supplication, ten such acts passed of which the Lords started
one; in 1533 – when the Act of Appeals took up much time – the
Commons initiated eight acts to the Lords' one.[86] In the spring
session of 1534, on the other hand, the twelve commonwealth
acts were equally divided between the Houses, though this was
achieved by the Lords in two cases substituting new bills for
those sent up from below.[87] For various reasons nine further bills
failed to pass in that session.[88] This massive production was
halted in the autumn session of 1534 when a heavy programme of
political legislation, including the Acts of Supremacy and Treason,
left no time for lesser matters. Even so, Cromwell had evidently
stirred up a lot of activity for the common weal before his thinkers
and writers came to rally round him; whether he initiated such
bills or helped more private enterprise to success hardly matters
in assessing his influence on the achievements of this Parliament.

The next vigorous shove came in 1536, especially in the last
session of the Reformation Parliament when thirteen reforming
acts reached the statute book, all but two of which started in the
Commons.[89] The eighteen months' interval since the last occasion
had evidently piled up some backlog, but one may fairly suspect
that the innovatory designs of the group now gathered around
Cromwell had to do with this intensification. The session witnessed two major reform bills – for land registration and poor

[85] Lords' bills: 22 Henry VIII, cc. 1, 2, 5, 6; Commons' bills: 22 Henry VIII,
cc. 7, 12, 14; cc. 1 and 2 revived old acts.
[86] 1532: 23 Henry VIII, cc. 1, 2, 3, 4, 5, 6, 7, 11, 13 (Lords' bill), 17; 1533:
24 Henry VIII, cc. 1, 2, 3, 4, 5, 6, 7, 10, 13 (Lords' bill).
[87] Lords' bills: 25 Henry VIII, cc. 1, 3, 6, 11, 13, 17 (cc. 3 and 13 really
originated in the Lower House); Commons' bills: 25 Henry VIII, cc. 2, 5,
7, 9, 10, 15.
[88] Vouched for by LJ. No doubt, if we had Journals for the other sessions of
the Reformation Parliament we should know about failed bills there, too.
In 1531, the session left behind sixteen bills that may be called for the
commonwealth (LP iv. 6043[3]); the difference between what was
attempted and what achieved underlines the importance of official steering.
[89] 27 Henry VIII, cc. 1, 4, 6 (Lords' bill), 9, 10, 12, 13, 14, 16 (Lords' bill),
19, 22, 23, 25.

relief – which, as we shall see, were certainly prepared by Cromwell's draftsmen. The new Parliament of June 1536, on the other hand, did little: apart from five Expiring Laws Continuance Acts (four moved in the Lords and one in the Commons),[90] only three not very significant acts were achieved, the two in the Lords being certainly official bills.[91] The reason is not far to seek. The Parliament of 1536 was a surprise to everyone: it was convened only because the fall of Anne Boleyn and the King's third marriage called for an urgent new Act of Succession. The Reformation Parliament finally went home on 14 April 1536, its dissolution offering sufficient proof that no one at that juncture intended to have another session so very soon; but almost immediately the King decided to proceed against the Boleyn faction, and on April 27th the new writs went out. Though there was time to prepare bills before the Parliament met on June 8th, and though a great many individuals did so for their own concerns,[92] the government evidently had no reform programme ready that time, and the slight achievement of that Parliament very probably indicates the degree to which even commonwealth legislation had become a matter of official initiative in Cromwell's hands.

In the three years before another Parliament met a good deal was done to reform the realm: those were the years of Cromwell's reform of the Church. But social and economic matters also received attention, and by 1539 the government again had a programme. Yet the problems of the Six Articles and the Proclamations Act absorbed so much time that only five commonwealth acts passed, three of them started in the Lords, by now Cromwell's own stamping ground.[93] Of the twelve bills which for one reason and another did not pass, six were certainly government measures and all but one were reintroduced in the next year when they became law.[94] That session of 1540 was to be the most

90 28 Henry VIII, cc. 1 (Commons), 2, 6, 8, 9.

91 28 Henry VIII, cc. 5, 14, 15 (Commons' bill).

92 There were 34 private acts in 1536, not only a large number in itself but rendered more remarkable still by the fact that the preceding session had passed 35. Some of them in both sessions were Crown bills, but the majority were entirely private. One may suspect a pile-up after the intensive public legislation of 1533–4 which may have left insufficient time for private bills.

93 31 Henry VIII, cc. 1, 2 (both Commons' bills and probably unofficial), 3, 7, 12 (all Lords' bills and certainly official).

94 See below, p. 154, for mispleadings, Trinity term, and limitation of pre-

productive of the lot, no fewer than twenty-six acts relevant to
our discussion being passed of which fifteen started in the
Lords.[95] The same number of bills failed of success, one of them
the only bill of that era which we positively know to have been
vetoed by the King.[96] To judge from the Lords' Journal, most of
the failed bills were introduced early in the session and contain
a high proportion of privately promoted ones; the bulk of the
successful bills came in late and were rushed through. It looks as
though government bills for the common weal had to wait for
the passage of the Subsidy Act and were possibly further put
back by the proceedings against Cromwell and the Cleves
divorce.[97] About that 1540 session there is an air of planners
finishing off a long developed and often delayed programme: the
Act for Pheasants and Partridges (32 Henry VIII, c. 8) occurred
first in Cromwell's notes in late 1533,[98] section 7 of the Customs
Act (32 Henry VIII, c. 14), raised in the Lords in 1534, was firmly
on Cromwell's programme by February 1536.[99] It is almost as
though Cromwell knew that 1540 would be his last Parliament.
At any rate, while reforms required the existence of a Parliament,
and while the vast preoccupations of the 1530's left insufficient
time for the full legislative programme put forward by both
planners and minister, Cromwell managed to use the time available to achieve a sizeable body of statutes of varying import and
weight. The last four Parliaments of the reign, without a Cromwell to plan programmes, witnessed a noticeable decline in this

scription. A bill against stealers of hawks' eggs was introduced in 1539 by
the duke of Norfolk and laid aside; it passed in 1540 (32 Henry VIII,
c. 11).

[95] Lords: 32 Henry VIII, cc. 1, 3, 5, 8, 11, 14, 20, 21, 33, 38, 41. Commons:
32 Henry VIII, cc. 2, 9, 12, 13, 16, 18, 19, 28, 30, 31, 32, 34, 36, 37, 42.
However, cc. 9, 12, 13 and 28 were really initiated in the Lords, the first
bills being replaced by new ones in the Commons.

[96] The bill for the Merchant Adventurers (*LJ* i. 162a). The bill for the
exposition of the statute concerning the export of cloth failed in the
Commons in 1540 but was passed in the next Parliament (33 Henry VIII,
c. 19); that for measures for coal and wood, which passed the Commons
in 1540 but lapsed in the Lords, became law in 1543 (34 & 35 Henry
VIII, c. 3).

[97] A good many of the successful bills reached Parliament after Cromwell's
fall, but since they included some known to have been planned by him
the programme for the whole session may fairly be associated with him.

[98] *LP* vi. 1381.

[99] *LJ* i. 59b; *LP* x. 254.

sort of activity.[100] It remains to consider just what was attempted and what achieved in the reform of the commonwealth.

[100] I calculate that those four Parliaments passed 12, 13, 7 and 14 acts dealing with commonwealth matters. Several of those passed were first planned by Cromwell, while a good few of the rest were only amendments to the legislation of his day.

5

AGRICULTURE, TRADE AND INDUSTRY

The reforms of Thomas Cromwell, essentially of a piece, may be conveniently classified in four categories. The most manifest, far-reaching and also successful touched the Church, both in its relation to the civil power and its function as a spiritual guide to the nation. This, the overriding concern of both reformers and government, cannot here be discussed, but we should always remember that a fundamentally religious conviction underlay the whole policy of renewal and revival. Secondly, a great deal was done to pull the parts of the realm together, by removing special privileges and constitutional diversities. The details of this are not unknown, though much could still be learned about Cromwell's Welsh and Irish policies; this, too, must for the moment be put aside. Thirdly, Cromwell saw the need to overhaul the central administration of the state, and whether one calls his achievements a revolution or not, it is established that he set about providing a more centralized, less personal, and potentially more efficient machinery. This I have discussed before.[1] And lastly, much attention was paid to the troubles of the commonwealth, our proper concern on this occasion. Reforms in this area concerned themselves with two distinct but closely related sets of needs: the socio-economic problems of society, and the insufficiencies of the law and its administration. The whole complex of measures and purposes was held together by a particular vision of the King's dominions as a self-contained entity capable of improving itself, an action of which it stood in much need and which was ultimately inspired by a concept of Christian living. The consistency and drive of this reforming activity have been somewhat obscured by the political dilemmas largely created by King Henry himself, by the practical difficulties in the path of reform, and by the undoubted and never solved problem of turning the intentions of the law into the facts of everyday life. More subtly the situation has been misunderstood because neither

[1] *The Tudor Revolution in Government* (Cambridge, 1953).

inspiration nor much of the detail was exactly new in the 1530's. For decades men of much insight or none had diagnosed the weaknesses of a society possessed of an indifferent Church, riven by economic ambition, and beset by disunities of all kinds; and in England, at least, positive proposals for reform had been evolving in many minds. It took no originality to pinpoint the area of required action. What was new in the 1530's were the will to transform ideas into fact and the energy which could undertake a simultaneous assault on all those long recognized needs. It is this that makes the decade so crucial – makes it a time of renovation and revolution.

Here, then, we are concerned only with the secular problems of society, with the reform of the commonwealth, a topic as diverse as social need itself and involving a lot of small things as well as some obviously important ones. Discussion of them is further hampered by the fact that others have been there before me. In particular, Whitney Jones has attempted to link contemporary analysis to contemporary measures, while many years ago Georg Schanz described the commonwealth policy at length so far as it touched trade and industry.[2] My excuse for traversing the ground once more must be that, concerned with much longer spans of time, they did both too much and too little. Schanz assumed the existence of a coherent government policy through several reigns; Jones assumed the direct relationship between advice-giving intellectuals and conciliar action. Both in consequence used all legislation without distinction to illustrate official activity. At the same time, neither looked in sufficient detail at the particular proposals and the particular laws. Concentration on Thomas Cromwell's ten years, and a better grasp of what actually happened in Parliament, should enable us to see what the commonwealth policy meant in practice, at a time when a commonwealth-inspired minister, possessed of knowledge, determination and political skill, tried to translate aspiration into achievement.

It took no special penetration at all to see where the major problem of the commonwealth lay: all one needed to do was to look out upon the roads of England. The country suffered from

---

[2] Jones, *Tudor Commonwealth*, chs. 6–9, each of which, however, runs over the full thirty years of his enquiry; G. Schanz, *Englische Handelspolitik gegen Ende des Mittelalters* (Leipzig, 1886).

vagrancy, as the age called it, or – as both we know and they fully recognized – from unemployment. Diagnosis had established the focal point sufficiently, most clearly perhaps in Clement Armstrong's treatise on how men were to be set to work.[3] Since Englishmen's employment was either in agriculture or in manufacture, it was necessary to restore the amount of tillage lost through conversion to pasture and the enhancing of rents, both of which had reduced the opportunities open to the small farmer, and on the other hand to assist the native manufacture of England's chief raw material of wool by limiting its export and encouraging the export of cloth. More briefly, Starkey said the same things.[4] Thus the necessary reforms included a check to enclosing, the restoration of tillage, the advance of the domestic textile industry, the promotion of overseas trade in manufactured products (especially cloth), and the rebuilding of decaying towns. More directly, treating a symptom rather than a cause, there were the victims of economic change themselves – the poor. Cromwell's administration tackled all these questions, with varying success.

The evils of enclosure were an old story; indeed, the operative act, 4 Henry VII, c. 19, had been passed as long ago as 1489. Attempting to freeze the agrarian scene by forbidding the pulling down of rural dwellings, it remained the fundamental measure against the conversion of arable to pasture,[5] but, of course, the real question was whether it could be enforced. Wolsey's one great attempt, the Enclosure Commission of 1517, had achieved very little, except to show that the acts had been generally ignored.[6] Since the policy was itself both crude and contrary to half-realized economic pressures, success had never been too probable, but this did not stop reformers from pursuing it. The Reformation Parliament at once had relevant bills before it; among the papers left behind by its second session were not only the copy of an earlier act dealing with the grievance,[7] but also

---

[3] *Tudor Economic Documents*, iii. 115–29.

[4] *Dialogue between Pole and Lupset*, 93–5, 156, 159.

[5] Modifications sharpening the penalties were introduced by 6 Henry VIII, c. 5, and 7 Henry VIII, c. 1.

[6] E. Kerridge, 'The Returns of the Inquisition of Depopulation,' *Eng. Hist. Rev.* lxx (1955), 212–28.

[7] Either Henry VII's act, or possibly 6 Henry VIII, c. 5 (made permanent by 7 Henry VIII, c. 1) which had tried to order the restoration of lost dwellings.

two bills touching the decay of husbandry, houses and tillage.[8]
These may have been private bills. Another, 'for the support and
augmentation of husbandry', was introduced into the House of
Lords in the spring session of 1534; but though the House read
what may well have been an official proposal four times, they
never got around to passing it.[9] However, in 1536, as the accum-
lations of this long Parliament were cleared away, Cromwell at
last obtained another Enclosure Act, 27 Henry VIII, c. 22. That
this was an official act emerges sufficiently from its tenor: the
failure of earlier legislation was ascribed to the fact that it
assigned the advantages of enforcement to the lords of the lands
who, unlike the King allegedly on his lands, had neglected their
duty. It was therefore enacted that the King could intervene to
exact the statutory penalties for enclosing when the immediate
lords failed to do so. This time Cromwell introduced the bill in
the Commons, but though he was careful to anticipate criticism
with a proviso stating that such temporary interventions were to
create no freehold in the Crown, he had to accept an amendment
which weakened the act by limiting it to certain shires. Even
though those named comprehended the major areas of enclosure,
they left out such sensitive spots as East Anglia and the Vale of
York.[10] Still, he had characteristically managed to change the
existing law in the direction of greater realism.

Cromwell's real interest, however, lay in tackling the subject
from, so to speak, the other end. It had long been recognized
that sheep-farmers evaded the enclosure acts by engrossing leasehold farms and removing the lands from tillage. In 1531, one of
Cromwell's advisers suggested measures designed to prevent
people from holding more land in this fashion than they could
employ in the maintenance of their households and to prevent
profiteering from sub-letting leaseholds.[11] These ideas may have
underlain the 'bill for farms' which failed to pass in that year's
session,[12] and they are hinted at in Cromwell's own preamble for
'an act for the maintenance of husbandry' of which nothing else

---

[8] *LP* iv. 6043(3).   [9] *LJ* i. 61b, 65b.
[10] Sect. 5 limited the act to Lincs, Notts, Leics, Warws, Rutland, Northants,
Beds, Bucks, Oxon, Berks, I. of W., Worcs, Herts, Cambs. It was added
in a different hand on the face of the engrossed bill and must therefore
be an amendment in the House of origin.
[11] *LP Add.* 754.   [12] *LP* iv. 6043(3).

survives.[13] Cromwell recited the effect of two statutes against the pulling down of rural dwellings (4 Henry VII, c. 19, and 7 Henry VIII, c. 1) and went on to complain that the law had been by-passed by people who accumulated 'small houses and lands of husbandry', leaving the dwellings to stand empty and decay, 'contrary to the true meaning and intent of the abovesaid good statutes'. Presumably the bill would have forbidden such accumulations. So far as we know, nothing was in fact attempted until the spring session of 1534 when Cromwell produced a major bill on the subject in which he planned to back the existing laws against enclosures with an effective limitation of the profits to be made from sheep-farming. The difficult parliamentary history of this bill has already been mentioned; now we must look in detail at what it tried to do and what was done to it.[14]

[13] SP 1/69, fos. 17–19 (*LP* v. 722[12]), a draft heavily corrected by Cromwell. This may well have been connected with the bill which lapsed in 1534.

[14] For this act, 25 Henry VIII, c. 13, see above, pp. 89–92. For the reconstruction of the original bill in the Commons I rely on Cromwell's letter to Henry VIII (Merriman, i. 373) and on a paper listing objections to 'the bill of farms if it should proceed as it is proposed' (SP 2/P, fos. 20–1 [*LP* vii. 58]). That this paper originated in the Lords and not (as Lehmberg supposed: *Reformation Parliament*, 189, n.1) in the Commons is proved by the fact that it was certified as collated with the original by Edward North, clerk of the Parliaments. It was evidently a copy made for Cromwell among whose papers it survived. One cannot, of course, be sure that it referred to the 1534 bill; it could be part of the lost story of the 1531 bill of farms. North became clerk on 14 February 1531 (*LP* v. 119[38]). In advising Henry of the bill, Cromwell said nothing of farms (i.e. leaseholds), but the lengthy complications of that part of the bill would sufficiently account for the omission. That farms as well as sheep were at issue in the 1534 bill is indicated by its title on the roll ('an act concerning farms and sheep'), and a somewhat incongruous clause for farms came back into what the Lords had left as a sheep bill only. We know that the bill ran into serious difficulties in the Lords who replaced the government bill from the Commons by one of their own. Yet of the two provisions listed by Cromwell they dropped only the very minor one touching the proportion of land to be kept under tillage. If this had been their only objection, replacement of the bill would be hard to understand; but if the original bill also legislated for farms in the comprehensive fashion indicated by the paper of protest, that severe reaction makes sense. We have a bill for farms and sheep which in the Lords was replaced by one for sheep only; we have a Lords' paper protesting against legislation concerning farms; it seems reasonable to connect the two. Moreover, the preamble of the Lords' bill continued to refer to the engrossing of farms, though there was nothing on this in the enactment. This shows that they followed the usual practice of basing their draft on the rejected bill and that the preamble was in Cromwell's original proposal.

The proposed legislation was drastic. It opened with a power-ful Cromwellian preamble which moralized on the needs of the commonwealth and introduced economic statistics to support its purpose. Greedy men 'to whom God of his goodness hath dis-posed great plenty and abundance of movable substance' have of late been gathering farms and turning them to pasture, with the result that food prices have risen disastrously; their motive has been the profitability of wool, greatly enhanced by the mono-polies so created. This is standard commonwealth stuff, well and concisely put, and the ensuing recital of figures for costs and prices, though unique in a parliamentary bill, was also a common-wealth speciality. The bill proposed three measures against such profiteers. No man was to own more than 2000 sheep. Lessees of leasehold lands must keep one eighth of them under tillage. No person is to possess more than two leaseholds each worth £5 a year and above. This last point, the crux of the matter, was qualified by complex concessions: for instance, farmers of two leaseholds worth £40 between them were free to lease an addi-tional uninhabited farm provided it was not attached to any 'manor, mese or cottage', and 'quillets' (small parcels) similarly unattached were altogether exempted from restrictions. But the main provision was rigorous, and any man possessed of more than the bill permitted had to rid himself of the surplus by sale or grant. The bill stopped a likely evasion by providing that a lease with a rent reserved on it should count as a farm vested in the lessor who thus would not be able to add to his holdings by creating fictitious leases of surplus land. The enforcement of the act was committed to justices of peace in Quarter Sessions.

Though the Commons passed this drastic bill, Cromwell's appeal to Henry to get it quickly through the Lords achieved nothing. The Upper House probably committed the bill to the judges[15] who received representations against the section on farms. The objections were many and varied – nineteen articles of them – but all designed to show that the bill would change the law (no wonder since that was its intention) and that the changes were 'unreasonable'. Poor men might either find themselves unable to acquire enough land to make farming possible, or else

---

[15] This I conclude from the fact that on its return from the Commons the bill was passed to a judge for a final check (above, p. 91).

be unable to rid themselves of land they could not afford to till. The objectors pointed out various ways in which the bill would harm titles of inheritance and rights to rents. Take the case of a lease by indenture, with obligation to perform covenants: if the lessee is forced to regrant the farm, both he and the new grantee will stand charged to the first lessor for the performance, 'which is thought that thereupon great trouble may ensue to the King's subjects'. Or if a copyholder for life or term of years grant under this bill all or part of the copyhold to another, this will be against the custom of the manor inasmuch as such regrants will be made without surrender in the manor court and therefore without entry on the court roll: in consequence of which the lord will lose fines, heriots and other profits. By the common law, a lease for life reserving a rent by livery of seisin created a freehold: the bill makes this a farm and thus destroys a freehold, an 'unreasonable' thing to do and a 'sore change in the law'. The alleged concessions were ridiculed since hardly any lands not attached to a manor or mese were to be found in the realm. As for empowering justices to enquire into offences under the act, this would lead to 'much trouble, unquietness, vexation, perjury, inconvenience'.

The protest was indeed formidable and shows the skill and power of a vested interest under attack. Told that the bill 'changeth the law of the realm and bindeth as well lords spiritual and temporal as all other inheritors and owners of lands and all other the King's subjects, and taketh away such liberties as they were and be entitled unto by the same law', their lordships not surprisingly took fright. Cromwell's great radical measure went into the discard, and in its place stood now a very simple bill retaining only the limitation on individual possession of sheep. This remained at 2000 per person. Some minor qualifications appeared: lambs under one year old were not to count, accidental excess such as flocks temporarily in the hands of executors or acquired by marriage was permitted for a year, sheep inherited by a minor were exempt during the minority. These were probably taken over from the original bill, as the committal of proceedings to justices of the peace certainly was. A proviso, on the other hand, which limited actions under the statute to within three years of the alleged offence, was more likely a Lords' amendment. But the core of the bill touching farms vanished, as did, perhaps by inadvertence, the provision for partial tillage of leasehold lands.

This mutilated bill now had to go back to the Commons where by this time opposition had had a chance to rally. There it was certainly committed, not yet a commonplace stage in the passage of bills, and the committee consisted of seven men who all sat for familiar sheep-farming counties – Wiltshire, Herefordshire, Warwickshire, Somerset, Berkshire and Hampshire.[16] The committee produced a paper of amendments as long as the whole Lords' bill, and this the House passed. But the amendments were not all of a kind; they show that Cromwell had to make further concessions but also that he fought back successfully. The first amendment stated that the bill was not to apply to lands held in inheritance, thus confining it to speculators in wool-growing who bought up leaseholds to run their sheep over, but this was no government defeat. The point needed inserting only because the Lords' revisions had removed all references to leasehold farms for which alone the restriction on sheep-owning had from the first been intended. A little clause to the effect that the 2000 were to be counted by the 'long hundred', on the other hand, did constitute a serious set-back for the commonwealth-men because it increased the permitted holding by a fifth, to 2400. However, section 14 of the act recorded a major victory for Cromwell, for it brought back the limitation on farms. This was now a brief and deceptively simple clause forbidding the acquisition, in future, of more than two farms unless all the properties lay within a man's parish of residence. The legal protests in the Lords had been heeded: the attempts to distinguish by value and to define lands of habitation had disappeared, the decision not to act retrospectively removed several objections based on compulsory sales, and the troubles resulting from the inability of villagers to rearrange holdings were avoided. In sum, the surviving provision, though much less embracing and drastic than the original proposals would have been, still put a stop to the worst form of speculation in leaseholds, the engrossing of farms by outside operators. Although the Lords added a further amendment which extended the concession for lands of inheritance to the lands

---

[16] Cf. Lehmberg, *Reformation Parliament*, 189 n.1. The list of names was certainly, not 'doubtless', a committee, for the clerk took care to use the dative case, writing 'Magistro Baynton' and so forth.

occupied by the clergy,[17] they did not renew their attack on the two-farms-only principle.

Thus Cromwell's chief assault on the problem recognized by all reformers as fundamental – enclosure, sheep-farming, and the consequent rise in rural depopulation and the price of food – suffered a notable setback at the hands of landlords' interests especially in the Lords but also in the Commons, giving some substance to Armstrong's later complaint that it was useless to attempt legislation against those evils in a body so constituted.[18] Nevertheless, the act was by no means a total loss, and Cromwell's influence in the Lower House even remedied some of the loss incurred in the Upper. The radical new ideas stayed in it: sheep-farming was made more difficult and less profitable, a much more promising way of tackling the problem than injunctions against enclosures had ever been. More especially, the act distinguished, as the bill had done from the start, between legitimate and anti-social pasturing, which the earlier acts had failed to do – one of the reasons for their ineffectiveness. If Cromwell could not get his full bill of farms, neither did the opposition succeed in removing all restrictions on the acquiring of leaseholds. The act remained in force longer than all the Tudor Enclosure Acts, and prosecutions under it are known as late as 1639. No one could really end enclosure and sheep-farming, and it would have been an economic disaster if they had; but Cromwell, with his expert advisers behind him, had at least achieved a partial answer along new lines which tackled the root problem rather than the consequential symptoms.

Neither Cromwell nor anyone else during his time attempted any other enclosure legislation: enough was on the book provided it was enforced.[19] But Cromwell realized that the problem of dilapidation and depopulation was not confined to the countryside. The state of England's towns appalled Starkey, used as he was to the splendours of continental cities: unlike the men of

[17] The clergy were already prevented from engrossing farms by an act of 1529 (21 Henry VIII, c. 13).

[18] *Tudor Economic Documents*, iii. 121. Armstrong may have had this session in mind, though in that case he displayed his ignorance of what really went on in Parliament by blaming the Commons alone.

[19] A bill 'for farms' passed the Lords in 1540 but was not heard of again after despatch to the Commons (*LJ* i. 131b): it may have been an amending bill intended to remove some of the limitations forced into the act of 1534.

France, Flanders and Italy, Englishmen seemed to prefer to let theirs fall to pieces.[20] A more careful analysis was provided by John Bayker, a 'poor artificer or craftsman' from Castle Combe in Wiltshire, who some time in the early or mid-thirties sent a long memorial to Henry VIII.[21] Basing himself on experience gathered in journeys all over England, he argued that landlords alone were to blame for empty houses and homeless men. By raising rents and especially entry fines, they were putting houses out of the reach of many; even those who could afford to pay had then nothing left over to attend to repairs. And when a house began to show neglect, the landlord would eject the tenant after a court action designed to make him do what his means simply barred him from attempting. In this manner, men lost their houses to join the wandering rabble on the roads, with robbery and murder and fornication as their sole employ, while the empty houses fell to ruin since landlords would neither repair them nor re-let at reasonable rents. Whole towns felt themselves in danger of decline; thus Bristol prepared a petition to the King which Cromwell corrected, lamenting the ruin of over 900 houses, ascribing it all to the decay of cloth-manufacture in the city and seeking relief from various financial burdens.[22] A draft bill among Cromwell's papers proposed to help towns by giving them a monopoly of all retail trade, under the control of the municipal authorities; some of its ideas became law in 1554, but Cromwell, probably wisely, ignored proposals which were both impracticable and unlikely to produce the desired benefits.[23] An obscure bill which would have further controlled retail selling by limiting certain goods to certain towns passed the Commons in 1540; but since it was not even read once in the Lords it is unlikely to have had government backing.[24]

[20] *Dialogue*, 92.

[21] SP 1/141, fos. 134–5 (*LP* xiii. II. 1229). The *LP* dating of 1538 is conjectural; Bayker's reference to the failure to enforce the 1531 Vagabonds Act suggests an earlier date.

[22] SP 1/236, fos. 346–56 (*LP Add*. 705). The petition may never, of course, have been presented. It was drawn up before there was any question of attacking monasteries, and the *LP* dating of 1530 may well be right. If so, Cromwell's part in this belongs to his private practice, but in any case it shows him to be familiar with urban problems.

[23] Cf. my remarks in *Bull. Inst. Hist. Res.* xxv (1952), 122–3. The idea that trade should be confined to towns was as old as Anglo-Saxon times (cf. H. Loyn in *England before the Conquest*, ed. P. Clemoes and K. Hughes [Cambridge, 1971], 122–3). [24] *LJ* i. 117a.

The problem of decaying towns had received attention before this: the Enclosure Act of 1515 had included town dwellings among those it protected, but only if they were in some way connected with husbandry.[25] This would not have done much good to Bristol's 900 houses once allegedly occupied by textile workers, or solved the problem of Bayker's untenanted hulks. In the 1532 session, a bill 'for the decay of houses' received one reading in the Commons, but that could have been a tillage bill.[26] Cromwell, in fact, did nothing until private enterprise had shown the way, but he then seems to have discovered an interesting parliamentary device to assist self-help. In 1534 both Norwich and King's Lynn obtained acts to help rebuild ruinous houses.[27] The acts are so different in form that a common origin is improbable, but both adopt the same essential principle, namely that the corporation may intervene to rebuild if the owners of the property have proved neglectful for a stated time. In the next session, a similar enabling act, privately promoted so far as appearances go, gave like powers to the municipalities of Nottingham, Shrewsbury, Ludlow, Bridgnorth, Queenborough, Northampton and Gloucester.[28] This is an odd gathering of towns: it looks rather as though the initiative may have come from the Welsh border country and that other towns may have joined in once the bill was promoted. And this is what really must have happened in 1540 when two virtually identical acts gave the same powers to, respectively, thirty-six towns all over the kingdom and twenty-two towns in the western parts.[29] The first took care of practically every town of any significance except London and those already equipped in 1536; the second listed twenty towns in Devon, Cornwall and Somerset, but added Maldon in Essex and 'the borough and shire town of Warwick'. These two, one may conjecture, had been too late for the drafting of the first bill. Though such portmanteau acts could have come out of private action, their common form rather implies government initiative. I suggest that we have here the appearance of a new device: that Cromwell proposed to encourage the rebuilding of towns by offering a place in officially drafted statutes to any municipality that wished to put its name down. After 1540, virtually all places of any size at all

25 7 Henry VIII, c. 1.
27 26 Henry VIII, cc. 8, 9.
29 32 Henry VIII, cc. 18, 19.

26 *LP* vi. 120(1).
28 27 Henry VIII, c. 1.

had the means to hand to remedy decay if they were willing to use it. This was a very sensible reform – much better than an act attempting the impossible by setting up a general rebuilding programme centrally organized. It put the force of government interest and the machinery of Parliament behind the needs of the locality and its ability to help itself. This body of legislation for urban renewal forms an interesting precedent for the local and private acts procedures of later days.

However, if towns were to be rebuilt their prosperity needed ✓ reviving, and altogether, if the economy of the country was to improve, the questions of manufacture and trade stood paramount, the more so because they offered a territory in which government action habitually participated and could reasonably hope to achieve things. Before we turn to this theme, it will be as well to get a subsidiary set of measures out of the way. As always, so also in the 1530's, a number of acts were passed to control individual trades and set acceptable standards of production and conduct. Both Schanz and Jones have ascribed them all to government action. The reality shows a more muddled picture. The session of 1531 left behind bills for cobblers, saddlers, tanners and fullers, on the face of it a concerted assault on major trades; but of these only the tanners' bill can reasonably be ascribed to the government: both the act of this session forbidding butchers to keep tanning houses and the act of 1533 (based on this unfinished bill) for controlling the making of leather, look like official bills.[30] There is no telling whether the bill for cardmakers, wiredrawers and pinners, left unfinished in 1532, originated with the government; the fact that it was never reintroduced weighs the other way. In 1533, the act for graziers was foreshadowed in Cromwell's notes,[31] while that for pewterers, as has already been said, was almost certainly private.[32] The act prohibiting the sale of foreign printed books, ostensibly to boost the native printing industry, might easily be read as a disguised form of official censorship; however, it was private in origin and presumably

[30] 22 Henry VIII, c. 6, was introduced in the Lords; 24 Henry VIII, c. 1, a Commons' bill, not only reads like an official act, but the bill was engrossed by the same hand as the Apparel Statute, c. 13, which was certainly official. Since this last started in the Lords, both bills were presumably introduced on parchment.

[31] 25 Henry VIII, c. 1; *LP* vi. 1381.

[32] 25 Henry VIII, c. 9; see above, pp. 80–1.

promoted by the printers themselves (most of whom, admittedly, were in touch with Cromwell).[33] The most interesting acts of this kind look to have originated outside government circles. The act for the proper dying of cloth (1532) imposed regulations so conservative, even backward-looking, that one feels some relief at being able to assign it to the dyers themselves; only old-established dye-stuffs were permitted, on the usual plea that certain technical innovations resulted in an inferior product, and the control over the process was entrusted to the Dyers' Company, with power to search.[34] In fact, the government do not seem to have been very happy with it. In 1533, Cromwell's papers included yet another bill on the same subject, and in 1534 a bill to repeal the recent act received two readings in the Lords.[35] This was one issue that Cromwell pursued no further. The act against fraudulent winding of wool, which caused some resentment in the industry, looks like a private bill – a very short act, without a preamble, and engrossed in an entirely unofficial hand.[36] The other act much resented by the clothing interests – that of 1536 setting standards in the manufacture of cloth – was also almost certainly not a government measure: its preamble embodied the standard merchants' complaints about the product they were expected to sell, and the readiness of the government to suspend the act by proclamation makes an official origin less likely.[37]

The decade witnessed some efforts to continue the central control over local ordinances which had been repeatedly legislated for since the reign of Henry VI, but the first bill, of 1531, which limited apprenticeship fees, was certainly of the Commons' own promotion,[38] while the much more effective amending act of 1536, which put a stop to obvious evasions, was introduced in the Lords by the lord chancellor and was official.[39] Some difficulties

---

[33] 25 Henry VIII, c. 15; the bill passed the Commons but was heavily altered in the Lords who, among other things, insisted on appointing a Council committee to control prices (*LJ* i. 60b, 65b, 66b, 69a–b, 74b). One may well guess that this arose from government intervention.

[34] 24 Henry VIII, c. 2. The bill was a Commons' petition and received the private act assent.   [35] *LP* vi. 299(xi); *LJ* i. 63b, 65b.

[36] 23 Henry VIII, c. 17; it started in the Commons.

[37] 27 Henry VIII, c. 12; cf. *TRP* i, no.175.

[38] 22 Henry VIII, c. 4, which starts 'prayen the Commons' still at this time a safe indication of source.

[39] 28 Henry VIII, c. 5; *LJ* i. 94a, 95a–b.

also attend upon the price-fixing statutes of the period, measures which one might really have supposed must have come from the government. The first act to attempt this kind of regulation was passed in 1533, and it has for good reason been read as a government bill: it took the same line as an ordinance of Wolsey's issued in 1529, and the government made every effort to get it applied.[40] However, the act was cast in the form of a petition and given the private act assent; moreover, it was soon amended by acts whose official origin is not in doubt. In 1534, additional enforcing machinery was created, but in 1536 another official act admitted defeat and abandoned price control at least until 1540.[41] Possibly all these measures were official – an effort to achieve by statute what proclamations and exhortations had failed to bring about – and certainly the policy proved over-ambitious, but the foundation act cannot be safely assigned to Crown initiative. The more general act of 1534 for a standing committee with powers to fix prices is even more puzzling.[42] The surviving bill, which reads official enough, was produced in the Commons; the Lords' Journal indicates that it was first introduced in the Lords but replaced in the Commons. And it was this seemingly unofficial replacement that became law.[43] A fortnight earlier, the Lords had rejected, after four readings, a bill dealing with butter and cheese only which the Commons had passed: presumably the bill on the subject which Cromwell on the eve of the session reminded himself to get engrossed.[44] The history of this important price-control statute is thus obscure, but it is evidently unwise simply to assume that it represented and embodied government policy.

These various controls, generalizing gild regulations and municipal ordinances, may thus well have owed as much to sectional interests as to Crown policy; and after all, they constitute a minor element in a policy concerned to assist the commonwealth. The real problem involved in the protection of manufacture and trade revolved around the measures to be taken to revive the making of cloth and ensure the best exploitation of England's

[40] 24 Henry VIII, c. 3; cf. R. W. Heinze, 'The Pricing of Meat: a study in the use of royal proclamations in the reign of Henry VIII,' *Hist. Journal* xii (1969), 583ff.; esp. 586–7.
[41] 25 Henry VIII, c. 2; 27 Henry VIII, c. 9.   [42] 25 Henry VIII, c. 2.
[43] Bill introduced and read three times, *LJ* i. 80a; returned from the Commons and again read three times (i.e. a different bill), ibid. 80b.
[44] *LJ* i. 73a, 74a–b; *LP* vii. 49.

strong position in that industry. This was a subject on which Cromwell received much advice. Clement Armstrong, in particular, thought he knew exactly what needed doing and very much resented the scepticism or silence with which his instructions were received. His rebuke to the neglectful minister, written early in 1536, was sorrowful.[45] He who for three years had been Cromwell's 'servant in mind' could but deplore the minister's failure to grasp 'the image of the King upbearing upon his shoulders the Church of Christ in his heavenly manhood which is signified in an ordinary seal of his head office'. The reference was to the sixty-pages long essay of repetitive and flatulent rhapsodies on the theme indicated in which Armstrong embodied his spiritual vision of Church and commonwealth, an essay which would have been longer still but for the blessed fact that, as he concluded, 'I make an end for lack of paper'.[46] Cromwell had good cause to ignore it, especially as one of its main threads was an obsessive hatred of intellectuals and scholars who with their reliance on book-learning were preventing the world from seeing the truth of Christ's reign, while its sole specific proposals touched the replacement of priests by deacons. But, as Armstrong pointed out in his letter of rebuke, he had gone on to work out practicable plans for achieving his devout purpose to 'help all people to live out of necessity and scarcity'. He knew how to do it, without it costing the King one penny: 'the order thereof is made in such a form that lacketh but the ministry to do it indeed'. Immediately he was referring to his now familiar treatises on the Staple and the restoration of tillage,[47] but at the same time he was also bombarding the King with pamphlets on the export of cloth, in English and Latin. Cromwell showed sufficient interest to have one of the Latin pieces translated by Ralph Sadler.[48]

---

[45] The letter, calendared under the wrong date in *LP* vii. 1689, is printed in R. Pauli, *Drei volkswirtschaftliche Denkschriften aus der Zeit Heinrichs VIII. von England* (Göttingen, 1878), 48–51. For the correct date cf. S. T. Bindoff in *Econ. Hist. Rev.* xiv (1944), 67.

[46] SP 6/11, fos. 103–33 (*LP* vi. 416). This treatise was written before Queen Catherine became Princess Dowager – probably in 1532.

[47] *Tudor Economic Documents*, iii. 90–129.

[48] A first Latin book is missing; it is referred to in SP 1/239, fos. 3–8 (*LP Add.* 918[1]). Ibid. fos. 10–12 (*LP Add.* 918[2]) is a part of a later Latin treatise translated in full in ibid. fos. 13–20 (*LP Add.* 918[3]). Armstrong's authorship emerges from the contents and various cross-references to earlier writings.

Armstrong's advice centred upon his dislike of the Calais
Staple which in his view was inhibiting the English cloth trade
by exporting raw wool to be manufactured by England's competitors. The Staplers were not doing even this to the best
advantage because, through inertia, they were selling more
cheaply than necessary and doing nothing to stimulate wool
production to the degree the market would bear. He wanted to
see all wool turned into cloth at home, and if there were to be any
exporting of raw wool the King was to take it into his own hands.
The King would be able to raise the price of fine wool at will and
increase his income from the customs by £20,000 a year. All this
was worked out with a wealth of figures untestable by us but
based on much experience and some research. It was also
Utopian, for (as Armstrong recognized) the rise of Spanish wool-
production had for ever destroyed England's monopoly. Armstrong was out of date: English cloth exports were going up
anyway, and the real problem concerned the kind of cloth that
could be exported. Everyone was agreed that the biggest profit
could be made from fully finished cloth, but those familiar with
the trade were well aware that what the continental market
wanted was white or unfinished cloth for the finishing trades of
Brabant. This was the point constantly pressed by the Merchant
Adventurers, the carriers (and beneficiaries) of that essential trade:
Netherlands purchasers 'will in no wise meddle with any cloths
that be dressed, unless they may have them at a price under the
foot'.[49] There was thus a fundamental conflict between the
theorizers who understood the superior value of selling manufactures and the exporters who understood the nature of this
sophisticatedly interrelated trade, and for the outcome it was not
without meaning that some twenty years earlier Cromwell had
himself been a merchant trafficking with the Low Countries. He
still kept in close touch with the Adventurers, especially through
Stephen Vaughan. As for the Calais Staple, his policy like that of
his predecessors was conditioned by the administrative principle

[49] Cf. the Merchant Adventurers' 'Considerations. . .how it were more for
the universal wealth of the realm of England to convey and send over the
sea to the marts accustomed cloths of all prices not dressed nor shorn,
than cloths dressed and shorn,' printed by Schanz, Handelspolitik, ii. 571–
573, from BM, Tib. D. viii, fo. 40. Cromwell's copy, endorsed by
Wriothesley, is in SP 1/236, fo. 203v (LP Add. 671[3]). Its existence
limits Schanz's tentative dating of 1514–36 to c. 1534–5.

that the Staple should be responsible for looking after the expenditure of that outpost. It thus had to be kept in being, incompetent though it always proved at the task. The policy was finally settled by Wolsey's Act of Retainer of 1527; Cromwell's characteristic modification confined itself to continuing the Staplers' charter from 1534 for short terms only, thus imposing a measure of control.[50]

The decade opened with attempts to prevent the export of unfinished cloth – attempts to impose a 'commonwealth' solution. Among the bills of the first two sessions of the Reformation Parliament was one for precisely this purpose, while two more were brought in concerning the Merchant Adventurers at least one of which, attacking their high brokerage charges, was very hostile.[51] The export of unfinished cloth was governed by an act of 1514 which permitted it provided the goods were worth not more than five marks the piece.[52] The Adventurers counterattacked with a series of protestations against their Hanseatic rivals,[53] for support in extending their Iceland trade,[54] and especially representing the case for liberating the export of unfinished cloth.[55] There is no sign that Cromwell ever seriously contemplated a total prohibition of this last, whatever memorialists might say about the best way of boosting England's textile industry. Instead he adopted a policy of offering encouragement to existing exports, in the circumstances the only policy likely to yield results. In September 1531, on the King's instructions, he prepared a bill for improving the customs revenue from kerseys, but this seems to have failed in a Parliament in which monopolistic merchants had a strong voice.[56] In 1536 he conceded something to the Merchant Adventurers by accepting their argument that inflation had rendered earlier levels of price limits out of date and raised the top price for exportable unfinished cloth to the £4 thought right by the company;[57] in 1540 he tried to resolve some difficulties that had arisen out of the legalistic evasions of

---

[50] *The Ordinance Book of the Merchants of the Staple*, ed. E. E. Rich (Cambridge, 1937), 9–11, 19.

[51] *LP* iv. 6043(3).

[52] 5 Henry VIII, c. 3, amending 3 Henry VIII, c. 7, which had set the limit at four marks.

[53] SP 1/236, fos. 198–201 (*LP Add.* 671[2]).

[54] *LP Add.* 873 (which gives the full text).   [55] Above, p. 113, n. 49.

[56] *StP* i. 381.   [57] 27 Henry VIII, c. 13.

the law (to the detriment of the Adventurers) though the bill
failed in the Commons and was passed only the following year,
after his death.[58] On the other hand, he did not accede to the
Adventurers' desire for preferential treatment and the elimination
of foreign competitors and never, for instance, attacked the
privileges of the Hanse.

Quite on the contrary, Cromwell believed in free trade (as the
age understood it) and soon developed plans to encourage alter-
native channels of trade. His preparations for the first session of
1534 included a note for 'an act that all strangers repairing to this
realm and conveying out of the same woollen cloths shall pay for
the same but English custom during the term of three years'.[59]
If such a bill was introduced it failed to pass the Commons; there
is no mention of it in the Lords' Journal. The idea was revived in
late 1535,[60] but again, if Parliament was asked to consider a
measure extremely distasteful to the powerful London interests
(though welcome to the wool producers and weavers because it
stimulated competition) we remain ignorant of the fact. This,
however, was one reform which Cromwell wanted urgently
enough to by-pass for once an obstreperous Parliament, and on
26 February 1539 a proclamation issued which put alien merchants on a level with natives for the payment of all customs
duties, that on raw wool excepted, for seven years.[61] The extremely pompous preamble expatiates on the King's deep thought
and great care in executing the office and duty of monarchs 'to
study, devise and practise...to advance, set forth and increase
their commonwealths committed to their cure and charges', a
phrasing which shows the stable whence it came; it also explained
that the King was generously willing to forego his lawful income
from customs duties in order to encourage 'traffic and commutation within this his grace's realm'. The obvious purpose of the
proclamation was to boost trade, but its full inwardness appeared
only a year later, with the great Navigation Act of 1540.[62] This
not only confirmed earlier acts for the encouragement of English
shipping and provided more detailed regulations and means of
enforcement, but also confined the benefits of the proclamation to

[58] *LJ* i. 139a–b; 33 Henry VIII, c. 19.
[59] BM, Titus B. i, fo. 161 (*LP* vi. 1381).
[60] *LP* ix. 725(ii).   [61] *TRP* i. 281–3.
[62] 32 Henry VIII, c. 14, certainly an official act introduced by the lord
admiral in the Lords (*LJ* i. 138b).

foreigners exporting goods in English ships. Thus it for the first time added inducement to command, a promising development – or it would have been if Cromwell's successors had managed to resist the violent protests that soon came from the Netherlands.[63] Indeed, Cromwell's protective care for the Merchant Adventurers extended even beyond his death. A bill touching them and presumably attacking them (perhaps the same that Cromwell had put aside eight years earlier) passed both Houses in 1540 but was vetoed by the King, the only bill so treated in that period, so far as the record goes.[64]

Thus Cromwell's policy for the cloth trade avoided the extravagances of his advisers, all of which would have led to serious conflict with various well-entrenched interests at home and abroad – quite apart from the political limitations imposed by the necessity to keep on terms with the emperor and the Netherlands – while yet he managed to offer considerable immediate, and very attractive future, hopes for an expansion of England's staple industry. He tried to assist employment in other ways. The act of 1533 for the sowing of flax and hemp, unquestionably a government measure, explained its motives: the import of linen benefited only 'strange countries', while the absence of any such industry in England was reducing opportunities for employment and causing people to live 'in idleness and otiosity'.[65] Its terms once again demonstrated the eagerness of these reformers to deal in fundamentals: Cromwell proposed to create the missing manufacture by supplying the raw materials. He tried to assist it further by abolishing a monopoly: the act of 1529, promoted by the London linendrapers, which tightly controlled the making of linens, was repealed in 1536 by a liberating act introduced by the government.[66] Possibly Cromwell also welcomed the extraordinary initiative of Anthony Guidotti, an Italian merchant long resident at Southampton where he had married the daughter of Cromwell's client Harry Huttoft. In 1537 or 1538, self-exiled to escape his creditors, Guidotti ran across twenty-four unemployed silkmakers at Messina and promptly despatched them to

[63] Schanz, *Handelspolitik*, i. 86ff.

[64] *LJ* i. 143a, 147a, 150a, 162a.

[65] 24 Henry VIII, c. 4. The act, introduced in the Commons, opens with the words 'The King's highness, calling to his remembrance', an unfailing sign of official origin.

[66] 21 Henry VIII, c. 14; 28 Henry VIII, c. 4.

Southampton to start their trade there.[67] He proposed to recruit more families in Northern Italy. Cromwell's reaction is not known, nor does any trace survive of those deluded immigrants, but at least the story shows what was thought to bring a man favour with Cromwell.

The mercantile interest engaged Cromwell's favourable attention on other occasions which demonstrate more clearly still that he listened to professional rather than learned advice. Inevitably he got involved with the mysteries of foreign exchange, another matter in which the national interest – the prevention of an outflow of good coin and specie – could be thought to conflict with that of merchants trading abroad who needed a free exchange.[68] For a long time and especially since Henry VII's day, attempts had been made to control the transmission of money abroad in cash and by letters of exchange) through the office of royal exchanger or keeper of the exchanges. From July 1511 this was held by George Ardisono or Ardeson, soon associated with a sinecurist courtier – from 1520, Thomas More. [69] Though the main purpose probably was the management of payments to the Curia, the London exporters, who had their own needs and arrangements, had always resented the monopoly. In 1531, government circles, including the King himself, grew very exercised over the drain of coin, and Cromwell was instructed to consult with the judges about the best way to arrest it. It may not have been without malice that he got More, keeper of the exchanges, to assemble, as lord chancellor, the committee of legal advisers who concluded that the necessary proclamation could securely rest upon an act of Richard II.[70] It issued three days later and

---

[67] Guidotti's letter is fully transcribed in *LP* xii. I. 689 (Italian version: badly damaged) and xiii. I. 560 (English translation in full). For the man and the missing silkweavers cf. Alwyn Ruddock, 'Antonio Guidotti,' *Proc. of the Hampshire Field Club* xv (1941), 34–42.

[68] For the full story cf. Schanz, *Handelspolitik*, i, ch. 5, esp. pp. 519–23; from a different point of view, and not always accurately, it is also told in R. H. Tawney's introduction to Thomas Wilson' *Discourse on Usury*, 137–44.

[69] Ardeson was a merchant of Genoa who received letters of denization in June 1512 (*LP* i. 1266[30]). He was appointed exchanger in July 1511 (ibid. 833[62]); in the following year he bought protection by admitting Sir John Sharp to a half-share in the patent (ibid. 1266[32]), and in 1520 Sir Thomas More replaced Sharp (*LP* iii. 1073).

[70] Merriman, i. 409–10, Cromwell to the duke of Norfolk, 15 July [1531]. This is the famous letter in which Cromwell expressed his pleasure at

prohibited all export of bullion; that this was understood to include transmissions by letters of exchange is plain from Edward Hall's account of the event.[71] If the proclamation is to be taken literally it imposed an absolute stop, though the old statute (which it recited) only confined such export to those specially licensed. In any case, the keepership of the exchanges continued in existence.[72] Thomas Audley inherited it, with the great seal, from Thomas More, and Ardeson survived into the 1540's. No doubt, exchange under licence therefore remained possible.

For the time being, the government, influenced by the expert opinion which associated bullion outflow and falling exchange rates with a free exchange, remained hostile to the mercantile interest. In 1536, they endeavoured to settle the matter by Act of Parliament. A bill for the exchanges passed the Commons, but after committal to the lord chancellor it disappeared in the Lords.[73] Audley, in fact, was defending the interest of his own office in keeping at least a licensed exchange going, for the bill apparently wished to terminate all such business. This emerges from a paper which lists possible objections and answers them.[74] To the point that the King would need foreign currency to pay his debts and other services it was replied that the King could always confiscate such money held by merchants. Ambassadors as well as 'students and travellers in countries' could use letters of credit arranging absolutely par exchanges in terms of bullion. Evidently, the purpose of the bill was to end exchange speculation. The fear that merchants and shippers would be driven to smuggle coin was somewhat optimistically turned aside: the

hearing that such proclamations needed no statute and were as good (in such cases) as Acts of Parliament. Thanks to *LP* viii. 1042, it has always been misdated into 1535. Schanz, *Handelspolitik*, ii. 631, unaware that the letter was Cromwell's, came nearer the truth by opting for 1530. The extraordinarily deferential tone of the letter, quite unlike Cromwell's attitude to the duke in the days of his own ascendancy, renders 1535 thoroughly improbable; 1531 is confirmed by the fact that the discussion recorded in the letter resulted in a proclamation (see next note) which simply embodied the opinion obtained by Cromwell from the judges. There is no other proclamation for the same purpose in the whole of the decade.

[71] *TRP* i. 199–201; Hall, *Chronicle*, 781.
[72] Schanz, *Handelspolitik*, i. 522, was wrong in thinking that Ardeson died in 1532 and that the office lapsed.
[73] *LJ* i. 95b, 99b.
[74] SP 1/141, fos. 242r–v (*LP* xiii. II, App. 27). *LP*'s 1538 is wrong: the bill of 1536 was the only attempt of the time to legislate for the exchanges.

offence could be readily detected, and besides, if merchants exported goods at the right price they would be able to deal successfully by a kind of refined barter. As for merchants' debts abroad and the activities of men who never dealt in manufactures (that is, currency speculators), these were the chief cause of 'the fall of the exchange' and deserved no consideration. Nor would the stop cause prices to rise in England, as some feared.

However, the bill failed, fortunately for England's export trade, and the government, a year later (8 July 1537) fell back on a modification of its purpose in a proclamation which, reciting a number of earlier acts, re-established the licence system and appointed persons unnamed (presumably the keepers of the exchanges) with whom offenders should compound. In other words, they had turned a blind eye to evasions for six years, but now, contrary to the merchants' desire, lowered the boom. For this proclamation, unlike its predecessor, took effect. Within a year Sir Richard Gresham, Cromwell's leading London contact, was expostulating against it, explaining how the stop of the exchanges had arrested trade and was in fact forcing merchants to smuggle gold, thus achieving the opposite effect to that intended.[75] Once persuaded, Cromwell did not hesitate – if indeed he had been behind the earlier policy. A few days after he received this letter, he got the Council to agree to a freeing of the exchanges until November 1st following, promising that the King would devise some final solution before then.[76] A week later, another proclamation seemingly addressed to London only removed both the time limit and the promise of future action, and the exchanges were entirely free.[77]

While Gresham might rejoice, the patentees felt differently: both Ardeson and Audley wrote urgently to Cromwell for compensation, the first in an attempt to prevent the freeing, the second after the event.[78] However, though Audley reminded the lord privy seal that in agreeing to the freeing the Council had advocated some compensation for the keepers, it does not look as though either of them got anything, rather an unusual event in sixteenth-century reforms which underlines Cromwell's single-

[75] BM, Otho E. x, fo. 45 (*LP* xiii. I. 1453); printed Schanz, *Handelspolitik*, ii. 632–3.
[76] *TRP* i. 265.   [77] Ibid. 266.
[78] *LP* xii. II. 140 (Ardeson); xiii. II. 240 (Audley: misdated by a year in *LP*). Audley's letter is printed in Schanz, *Handelspolitik*, ii. 635.

mindedness once he had made up his mind. Fears of a bullion-drain produced the inhibition of 1531 which did not, however, end both evasion and licensed exchanging through the proper officers. In 1536, continued bullion exports, an adverse exchange rate, and the anti-mercantile bias of expert advisers with their customary fixed idea about 'speculators' culminated in a bill in Parliament which was frustrated by Lord Chancellor Audley's ability to protect his interests even against Cromwell. A situation composed of an impossible prohibition and winked-at necessary evasions was hardly likely to appeal to Cromwell, and at first he tried to satisfy Audley by re-establishing his profitable office, giving the chancellor and his working partner Ardeson a chance to make more in compounding for past offences. This moved the merchants to mobilize Gresham and through Gresham his friend the minister, and this time they won because they could prove the effect that the stop had had on trade. It is arguable that by freeing the exchanges Cromwell did more for the export trade than by all the legislation designed to encourage it directly. Here he listened to the Adventurers; with respect to customs duties he offended them; what links his measures is a general policy to make trade as free and current as possible.

Gresham's letter of July 1538 contains another reminder of the ways in which Cromwell was eager to promote reforms designed to help the mercantile community and with it, as he saw it, the common weal of England. In addition to appealing for a free exchange, Gresham also submitted his famous proposal for a London *bourse*, including even drawings for a suggested building. So much is well known; what is not so well known is that in 1539 Cromwell himself introduced a bill into the Lords to turn the dream into reality. But though he got it through the Upper House it failed in the Commons, perhaps for lack of time, and he made no second attempt in the following year.[79] The Royal Exchange was to be the creation not of Richard Gresham but of his son Thomas, and its fame accrued to the reign of Elizabeth, not to that of her father when yet his greatest minister saw the value of the idea sufficiently to put his own influence behind it at a time when far too many matters of weight were distracting him – among other things, his own struggle for survival. It is also

[79] *LJ* i. 116b, 117b. But cf. Schanz, *Handelspolitik*, i. 523 n.1, who did spot the reference.

mildly interesting to note that if Cromwell had had his way the Royal Exchange of London would have been a parliamentary creation.

Trade was not the only enterprise to receive Cromwell's attention. Other important social concerns were reformed by the Act for Barber-Surgeons of 1540, with its extremely commonwealth-style preamble,[80] and by the comprehensive sumptuary law of 1533.[81] Sumptuary legislation was a bee in the reformers' bonnet to whom it represented an essential element in a stable social order, though, of course, it had already had a lengthy history before Cromwell appeared on the scene.[82] A bill on the subject was among those Cromwell was ordered to prepare for the session of 1532, but it proved too big a measure that time, receiving only a first reading in the Commons.[83] In the next session, Cromwell had it first introduced in the Lords, and it became law as an Act of Apparel.[84] Earlier acts had only spoken very briefly of the impoverishment of individuals given to excessive luxury in dress; Cromwell's preamble lamented the 'notorious detriment to the common weal' and 'the subversion of good and politic order in knowledge and distinction of people according to their estates', just the sort of phrase one would expect from his circle. In his hands sumptuary legislation ceased to be the means for saving fools from extravagance and became an instrument of social control, a very commonwealth kind of attitude.

Cromwell also wished to preserve the realm's assets. The 1532 session gave two readings to a bill to save the natural regeneration of woodlands, and Cromwell tried again in 1540, the bill receiving three readings in the Lords when he was no longer there; but success had to wait for the Parliament of 1543.[85] He did rather better with the conjoint problems of riverways and fen-drainage. The 1532 Act for Commissioners of Sewers – the act which laid the real administrative foundation of the system that was in due course to clear England's marshlands – was his,

[80] 32 Henry VIII, c. 42, an official act expressing the King's considered intention to take action.
[81] 24 Henry VIII, c. 13.
[82] Jones, *Tudor Commonwealth*, 93–4, 102; W. S. Holdsworth, *History of English Law*, iv (London, 1924), 405–6.
[83] *StP* i. 382; *LP* vi. 120(1).
[84] 24 Henry VIII, c. 13.
[85] *LP* vi. 120(1); *LJ* i. 156b, 158a; 34 & 35 Henry VIII, c. 17.

planned the year before and introduced into the Commons.[86] Cromwell, in fact, must have been something of an expert on drainage problems: the transfer in 1525 of the lands of Lesnes Abbey in Kent to Wolsey's collegiate foundations had involved him in a good deal of work about the marshes of Plumstead and Woolwich.[87] He may have been behind the act of 1531 intended to drain those marshes: it sounds official rather than private.[88] A petition from the fishermen of the river Thames, protesting against 'extortioners' who used various devices to take fish out of the river above Staines may have moved him to plan a bill banning all weirs and watermills, but this came to nothing.[89] The only successful preservation act for fish, passed in 1534, was probably a private bill introduced in the Commons; in fact there were two such bills of which the Lords passed one, returning the other to the Lower House where it was understandably abandoned.[90]

These and similar particular acts are the common coin of any active administration's legislative programme and, even when officially promoted, no doubt at times originated in sectional representations of which we know nothing. Nevertheless, the accumulation of them, together with the frequent occurrence of determined 'commonwealth' propaganda in preambles, mark the work of the Cromwell administration as both more planned and more intensive than usual, to say no more. The intended crown of his legislation for the common weal, however, was a different matter altogether. The reforms in agriculture and commerce were designed to stimulate employment and assuage the consequences of distress. This still left the hard core of pauperism and vagrancy, Tudor England's besetting problem. As is well known, Cromwell was responsible for the first really thoughtful poor law which attempted to provide relief to the victims of society rather than merely punish those whom destitution made a social danger.[91] As has also been known for a little time, the act had a

---

[86] 23 Henry VIII, c. 5; *StP* i. 382.
[87] Cf. *LP* v. 1631.   [88] 22 Henry VIII, c. 3.
[89] SP 1/239, fo. 277 (*LP Add.* 1048); *LP* x. 254.
[90] 25 Henry VIII, c. 7; *LJ* i. 73b, 74a, 78b, and 74b, 75a–b, 76b. The dropped bill apparently concerned itself only with salmon; the act passed dealt also with eels; the former had a schedule added in the Lords of which there is no sign in the act.
[91] 27 Henry VIII, c. 25.

more complicated prehistory than appeared on the face of it. It originated in a draft bill prepared by Cromwell's staff which proposed to tackle all aspects of the problem.[92] The ablebodied unemployed were to be set to work on such useful enterprises as the rebuilding of harbours, highways and water-courses; they were to receive wages and maintenance and medical care; and the scheme was to be financed by a graduated income tax. The sick and aged were to be relieved by the alms of the parish, voluntary but organized. The draft provided extensive machinery, from local overseers of the poor to a standing 'council to avoid vagabonds' which supervised the whole grandiose scheme and employed the directors of individual works. This was no pipe dream. The draft rested both on general considerations put out by the theorists and on an acquaintance with relief schemes tried abroad,[93] and it was carefully worked out in stages. Nor was it pared down to its ultimately modest remnant before being tried on Parliament, as I had once supposed. The surviving draft was not ready for introduction – the rates of the income tax, for instance, are left blank – but a bill embodying all its major ideas was put before the Commons in March 1536. Thomas Dorset, a priest visiting London, heard the details from a burgess of the Parliament: at this stage they still included the scheme of public works and other points not in the act as passed. The same information reached the imperial ambassador.[94]

It appears that Cromwell, as well he might, expected trouble for his revolutionary poor law. Once again, as for the Sheep Act, he mobilized Henry VIII to help through a commonwealth measure, this time surprisingly in the Commons. On Saturday, March 11th, the King came in person to the Lower House to present the bill, with a well-rehearsed speech urging members to consider it with care: 'he would not, he said, have them pass on it nor on any other thing because his grace giveth in the bill, but they to see if it be for a common weal to his subjects and have an

---

[92] The draft, first adumbrated in the 'comprehensive draft' of 1534 (above, pp. 73–4) is discussed at length in G. R. Elton, 'An Early-Tudor Poor Law,' *Econ. Hist. Rev.* 2nd series, vi (1953), 55–67. That the taxing of the nation should end in 1540 was apparently suggested at some stage during the working out by another member of the planning staff (SP 1/99, fo. 228 [*LP* ix. 1605]).

[93] Starkey, *Dialogue*, 160.

[94] *Three Chapters of Letters relating to the Suppression of Monasteries,* ed. T. Wright (Camden Society, 1843), 38–9; *LP* x. 494.

eye thitherward'. He would return on the 15th 'to hear their minds'.[95] The manoeuvre failed. In fact, it would appear that opposition was immediately so great that the government withdrew the bill and substituted the present weakened version. The Original Act extant is a unique document: not the usual parchment sheet but a 'book' made by folding two parchment sheets and stitching them inside each other. The handwriting is that of a member of Cromwell's secretariat.[96] The bill as prepared ran down to section 20 which still starts with the word 'finally'. It was possibly committed and certainly modified, for the next three clauses (one proviso and two further enactments, all in the nature of minor amendments) were added in the 'book' itself, two of them in a hand which recurs entering amendments on other bills and may well have been that of the clerk of the House. Thus it went to the Lords who added five further provisos. But none of those amendments seriously affected the act which stood essentially in the substituted form presented by the government.

Even so, this was not the end of the troubles encountered by this surely commendable measure. Section 20 limited its duration till the end of the next Parliament, so that if it was not to lapse it would have had to be renewed in the Parliament of June 1536. And it appears that the government tried but failed to get this renewal. One of the Expiring Laws Continuance bills of 1536 was rejected in the Lords, or so the Journal says.[97] Yet the bill in question did become law, as 28 Henry VIII, c. 6. This renewed, among other things, the Beggars Act of 1531 but not that of 1536, both up for expiry. The most likely explanation of this confusion is that both poor laws were included in the Continuance bill, but

---

[95] Cf. Dorset's letter. There has been a long-standing supposition that the bill Henry was presenting was that for the Dissolution (cf. M. D. Knowles, *The Religious Orders in England* [Cambridge, 1959], iii. 291–2). But Dorset, who reports the scene, went on at once to describe the poor bill and says not a word about monasteries. Chapuys' report that the King had proposed such a bill to the Parliament lends further support, even though he might have been speaking loosely. And Henry's reported words about the common weal fit the poor bill better than the other. Lastly, the Dissolution bill, cast in the form of a petition from both Houses, can hardly have been introduced by the King.

[96] This militates against Lehmberg's theory that the bill was produced in a Commons' committee (*Reformation Parliament*, 232). Other bills were committed, but engrossment always took the standard form. The form of this Original Act cannot really have been shaped in Parliament.

[97] *LJ* i. 89b.

that the Lords refused to pass the latter until the 1536 poor law
was taken out of it. Technically, therefore, that act lapsed, nor
was it explicitly renewed in 1539.[98] Thereafter its fate was
peculiar. One line of evidence suggests that it had ceased to exist;
another that it stayed on the book. The poor law of 1547 repealed
all earlier acts without specifying which were intended; when
this in turn was repealed in 1549, only the act of 1531 was declared
revived.[99] This law finally disappeared in 1624,[100] but on that
occasion nothing was said of the 1536 statute which thus might
be thought to have been technically dead from the moment that
renewal was first refused to it. However, a proclamation of 1538
enjoined the enforcement of statutes (in the plural) touching
vagabonds, in clear distinction from the earlier proclamation of
February 1536 which, before the second law was passed,
referred to only one such statute.[101] And indeed, in the view of
the law Cromwell's poor law remained in force, for it was thought
necessary to repeal it in one of the great cleaning-up operations
of the nineteenth century.[102] This hesitant treatment of a relatively mild though promising measure is difficult to understand.
Its troubles stemmed from the opposition to renewal in 1536:
why was that opposed? Of course, Cromwell's original bill tried
for such a lot of things and was so revolutionary in its implica-
tions that resistance to it does not surprise, but the substitute bill
did not deserve to run into such obstruction. Presumably what
really killed the first bill was the income tax proposed, while the
enacted bill possibly continued to displease because it tried to
provide for a poor rate. This was so far to be voluntary, but if
opposition feared the worst it proved, though selfish, also far-
seeing: the compulsory poor rate which arrived in the end rested
on the beginnings made in this act.

For, as has been said, despite its dubious history in continuance
and repealing acts, Cromwell's poor law must be treated as real
and existent. The minister himself evidently felt unhappy about

---

[98] 31 Henry VIII, c. 7: although the editorial note includes the poor law
of 1536, it is not mentioned in the text.

[99] 1 Edward VI, c. 3; 3 & 4 Edward VI, c. 16.

[100] 21 James I, c. 28.

[101] *TRP* i, nos. 132, 163. For the correct date of no. 132, cf. below, p. 165.

[102] 26 & 27 Victoria, c. 125. Since the 1536 act was explicitly declared to
be in augmentation of that of 1531, it is just possible that in the sixteenth
century references to the latter were deemed to include the former.

the situation and in 1539 once again contemplated 'a device in Parliament for the poor people of this realm'.[103] Perhaps he hoped to try once more for the full effect of the great draft law (and for that very reason did not bother to get the actual act continued?); the draft was assuredly not forgotten, since the first effective national scheme, that of 1572, though it attempted much less, showed in its phrasing a clear acquaintance with it.[104] Cromwell, in 1539, abandoned his intention. Nevertheless, by his care to be ready in 1536 with a second bill he had saved certain things: the idea of finding work for the able-bodied, the injunction against indiscriminate almsgiving, and the collection of a voluntary poor rate, all points to be taken up and developed in later legislation. That was all he could get the House of Commons to accept, despite the King's personal intervention. He had lost the chance of revolutionizing the whole treatment of poverty and unemployment, but he still left on the statute book the foundation of the relief organization which in the end was to serve the country quite well for two hundred years.

Of course, there were notions and plans about which came to nothing. Several of them displayed that touching faith in the power of law to rule human nature which is the hallmark of earnest reformers. A paper of bills proposed for the session of 1531 – a serious document some of whose suggestions came to leave their mark – wished to stop all poorish persons from gambling.[105] It set the lower limit of the ability to afford such diversions at £20 a year out of lands or fees and made some concessions: wagers were permitted at the national sport of archery, and so were bets for food and drink to be consumed on the spot. Starkey, too, disliked the gambling habit, though he inclined to blame rich men worst, and Cromwell acted to the extent of trying to enforce the existing laws against unlawful games and preparing the way for the comprehensive act of 1541.[106] But he refused to set an income limit on gambling. This was not the only proposal for an unworkable law. Starkey and Rastell, thinking quite independently, agreed that England was underpopulated, really a curious idea for them to have since they also recognized, with many others, the need to find employment for the people that did exist. Starkey spent much space on the

---

[103] *LP* xiv. I. 655.   [104] 14 Elizabeth I, c. 5.
[105] SP 1/237, fo. 80 (*LP Add.* 754).   [106] *Proc. Brit. Acad.* liv (1968), 183.

need to encourage marriage among temporal and ecclesiastical persons alike,[107] and Rastell likewise asked for an act 'that priests may have liberty to have wives'.[108] Both were less concerned to avoid fornication than to increase procreation. The influence of this line of thought may be traced in the tentative moves towards ending clerical celibacy, moves which the King personally terminated in 1538.[109] Eugenic principles inspired the suggestion that a statute should bar boys from marrying before puberty, while strong and potent men should be prevented from wasting themselves on old widows (as many did, for money's sake).[110] That same set of proposals, which certainly came from within the circle of Cromwell's advisers, also included a bill to stabilize the social structure: mercantile wealth was to be employed only in trade and not in buying land, craftsmen were to practise in towns and not to take farms, and no merchant was to own land worth more than £40 a year. Whether, with Plucknett,[111] one should see here an instance of a supposedly serious intention on the part of King and government to freeze society may well be doubted; at any rate, no actual proposal ever attempted anything remotely of the sort. Really bright and extravagant ideas, singularly unaware of the realities of life, found no response in Cromwell.

Less striking but rather more significant are bills vainly attempted in Parliament – though, of course, we know nothing of what was tried in five out of the nine sessions that concern us. In early 1534 the Lords passed a bill to bar persons with less than a certain income from land (we do not know the figure) from keeping hunting dogs and greyhounds; this disappeared in the Commons who represented the less affluent owners of hounds.[112] This bill may have been the product of private enterprise – some nobleman's pride of place mingling with the supposed dangers to the countryside of too many hounds – but the grievance was genuine. Some four or five years later, one Robert Pye, going about the country, reported to Cromwell that the people especially complained of the number of hounds kept by gentlemen and their tenants. Food that should sustain the poor went to feed those dogs instead, and the excuse that without them foxes would kill lambs was rubbish: where a fox might take two lambs

[107] Ibid. 182.
[108] SP 1/85, fo. 100 (LP vii. 1043).
[109] Above, p. 54.
[110] LP ix. 725(ii).
[111] Trans. Royal Hist. Soc. (1936), 123–4.
[112] LJ i. 69a, 75a, 76a–b.

in a night, greyhounds were known to have killed a score of sheep in the same time.[113] Perhaps Cromwell remembered the fate of the 1534 bill; if I have read him aright, he would in any case have had his doubts about this kind of selective attack on social habits; nothing was done. In 1539, we find the Lords blocking a Commons' bill for the supply of bowstaves on the interesting grounds that they wished to have the merchants of the Hanse consulted first; probably a piece of economic chauvinism was averted by government intervention.[114] The House also rejected a bill for pewterers introduced by the lord chancellor; this, per contra, looks like the victory of a lobby.[115] Not strictly relevant here is another government defeat. It would seem that Cromwell was concerned about the nature of holy orders, but a bill for the ordination of priests which he himself presented was slily referred to his personal opponents, Tunstall and Gardiner, and not heard of again.[116] Perhaps we should suppose that the Edwardian Ordinal had its origin in the vicegerent's mind, but 1539 was no time for radical reform in religion.

It was the long and busy session of 1540 which yielded the largest number of failed bills for the common weal. The Commons passed bills for bakers and brewers, for swans, for establishing uniform measures for coal and firewood, and against the sale of hides except in market towns: all these the Lords allowed to die.[117] They themselves passed what looks like a useful anti-pollution bill to prohibit the washing of linen and canvas in running water (it failed in the Commons), briefly considered one for clothmaking in Yorkshire, and rejected one concerning the tin-manufacture of the south-west.[118] There is no telling, of course, how many of these proposals – ordinary enough, but part of the reforming activity of those years – originated with the government. Possibly none did, though this would have been contrary to the experience of the decade which had witnessed so deliberate and detailed an attempt to survey all the needs of the commonwealth.

[113] SP 1/156, fos. 106v–107 (*LP* xiv. I. 810).   [114] *LJ* i. 109a, 110b.
[115] Ibid. 112a.   [116] Ibid. 115a.
[117] Ibid. 137a; 144a, 146a; 148a, 149a; 152a–b.
[118] Ibid. 157a–b; 130b; 131a.

6

LAW REFORM

In one sense, just about all Tudor reforms may be called reform of the law; since government operated under the symbol of the application of the law, all change was change in the law. More particularly, the subjection of the Church to the royal supremacy was in itself a major legal rearrangement and had a good many consequences of the same kind. However, I shall here confine myself to law reform proper, to changes in the administration of the law and in its substance. There were plenty of ancient griev-ances, often repeated, concerning the law and its practitioners, and although in the early Reformation rather more is heard of the shortcomings of the spiritual courts the common lawyers were by no means immune.

Complaints about the courts of the Church were voiced in the Parliament of 1529; two and a half years later, they emerged in the Commons' Supplication against the Ordinaries, linked there with other grievances.[1] The laity resented action at the instance of the court (*ex-officio* proceedings), heavy fees and long delays, and it was freely asserted that practitioners in the Courts Christian obtained work by corruptly initiating process against innocent men. The whole system, being both alien and papal, lay exposed to a double attack from nationalists and royal suprem-acists. That representative common lawyer, Christopher St German, wished at least to restrict the operations of the rival juris-diction, and Cromwell's planners included among their notions a proposal that at any rate matters touching the temporalities

---

[1] My remarks in *Eng. Hist. Rev.* lxvi (1951), 507–34. The final form of the Supplication is printed in *English Historical Documents 1485–1558*, ed. C. H. Williams (London, 1967), 732–6. For a discussion of the actual behaviour of the Church courts, which concludes that it was their effectiveness that was resented while some specific complaints were quite unjustified, cf. M. Bowker, 'Some Archdeacons' Court Books and the Commons' Supplication against the Ordinaries of 1532,' *The Study of Medieval Records: Essays in Honour of Kathleen Major,* ed. D. A. Bullough (Oxford, 1971), 282–316.

of the Church should be tried at common law.[2] Henry VIII's attack on Rome seemed in fact to offer a splendid opportunity for at last resolving the conflict of jurisdictions and laws. A draft bill of uncertain date proposed an extensive reform of the Church courts.[3] It prohibited all actions *ex officio* except in heresy cases, extended the canon law's principle that forty years constituted prescription to seventy, authorized actions by *quare impedit* against bishops who needlessly delayed instituting patrons' nominees to livings, ordered money obtained from the commutation of penances to be devoted to charitable purposes and the upkeep of churches, and committed the enforcement of these regulations to Quarter Sessions. Another hand – quite possibly that of Richard Riche, solicitor general from 1533 – added a further paragraph forbidding the payment of double tithe, that is predial tithe rated per acre and in addition tithe on the cattle raised on those same acres. This point was made briefly in the Supplication and may have been added to the bill after a reading of that protest. As in so many Cromwellian productions, the fierceness of the preamble was not fully matched by the careful particulars of the enactment, but the bill if passed would certainly have invaded the province and liberties of the courts spiritual.

There were other people who wished to go further. A paper of suggestions, convinced that the clergy, so much like lions in defence of their privileges, would if treated firmly behave like meek sheep, stressed the need to review the whole problem of the Church's claim to jurisdiction.[4] While the clergy had 'such power to correct the people' few of them would attend to their proper tasks of 'preaching, teaching and good example giving'. The writer thought it a good idea to remove at least some of the jurisdiction hitherto exercised by the Church: in that way the clergy might be taught that they enjoyed their remaining powers

---

[2] Above, p. 72.

[3] SP 2/M, fos. 23–6 (*LP* v, App. 28). The date of this draft may be as early as 1529 or as late as 1535. The *LP* dating rests on the assumption that it was connected with the agitation of 1532, which may be true. But so far as we know, that agitation confined itself to petitioning the King, nor does the draft bear very closely on the grievances listed in the Supplication. The only major point the two have in common touches the initiation of cases *ex officio*, but the draft's proposals would not have succeeded in solving the problems raised by the Supplication.

[4] SP 1/99, fos. 227–8 (*LP* ix. 1065). The conjectural date 1535 is probably correct.

by the sufferance of King and Parliament and not by 'any right that they may claim therein by the law of God or by any other way'. He suggested that for a start three things might be reserved from the Church courts – dilapidations, simony, and the trial of laymen charged with violence against priests – and proposed that immediately an act should extend all spiritual jurisdiction only to the end of the next Parliament, so that the whole problem could be thoroughly reviewed before then. He evidently held the highest possible opinion of the powers of statute.

Attacks of this kind did not, of course, go without an answer. The ordinaries' first reply to the Supplication not only refused to budge on a single point but also ranged more widely even than the protest it rebutted in defending the spiritual jurisdiction against every possible imputation.[5] The Church was not going to surrender its most positive, if perhaps least Christian, function without a determined fight. In early 1535 a defender of that jurisdiction drew up an extraordinary paper which attempted to combine unrelenting maintenance of all claims with reforms that would make the continued existence of the Church courts tolerable. Although the last part is now missing, there are sixty-one pages left, and somewhat strange reading they make.[6] Though there is no reason to think that Henry had anything to do with what can hardly have been an official scheme, it is cast in the form of an edict issued by the King and may have been intended for endorsement by him. The bulk of it touches regulations to be observed by the Church courts. They are to adopt the English new year (March 25th) and to abandon dating by years of indiction and pontificates; years A.D. and regnal years only are to be used. Officers of the courts, especially notaries, are to be licensed under a royal seal and to swear an oath, which is recited, to serve the King. Lengthy provisions clarify the course of appeals, allegedly somewhat uncertain since the two parliamentary attempts to settle it,[7] establish a very detailed scale of fees for all purposes, settle the rules governing the activities of proctors, and fix time limits for all stages of suits.

In the middle of this painstaking detail, which might appear

---

[5] Gee and Hardy, 154–76.
[6] SP 6/5, fos. 2–31 (*LP* viii. 296). The document recites the Act of Supremacy as though it had recently passed.
[7] 24 Henry VIII, c. 12, and 25 Henry VIII, c. 19, sects. 4–6.

as a genuine and officially sponsored reform, there occurs a sudden defence of the liberties of the Church, with an appeal to Magna Carta and later confirmations, which reads oddly when put in the mouth of the man who was so notoriously destroying those liberties:[8]

> In so much as the noble of memory Henry III, Edward I, and divers other our noble progenitors and ancestors, kings of this realm, have granted unto God and the Holy Church of England, and confirmed by sundry their charters, as also we ourself, in semblable manner, have granted and do confirm for us and our heirs that the Church of England shall be free and shall have the whole rights and her liberties unhurted, it is expedient that we do show what immunity, liberty and exception the Church and clergy of England hath both in their persons, places and causes from our jurisdiction and power secular.

The King is then made to explain that the word clergy derives from a Greek word 'cleros', meaning 'lot', from which it follows that they are elect and 'of another sort from our lay people'; they ought to be 'emancipate to divine service and to give themselves to contemplation, prayer and study of divine Scripture as clerks devout to God...And thus doing they do enjoy much liberty and exemption'. All secular courts are therefore forbidden to attack any ecclesiastical person – 'priest, deacon, subdeacon, clerk or the least minister in the Church' – without special royal licence. All spiritual causes and those involving clerks, even 'though the causes be criminal', are reserved to the Church courts. The rights of sanctuary in churches and churchyards are maintained except in cases of heresy and treason. Causes spiritual are listed: matrimony and divorce, sacrilege, heresy (subject to observing the act of 1534 which regulated process),[9] simony, excommunication, breaches of contracts made in spiritual courts, adultery, incest and fornication, withholding of tithes and offerings or other rights of the Church, probate, maintenance of benefices and the fabric thereof, violence against clerks, defamation and slander. This is as comprehensive a list as anyone could produce; it includes all the particulars often objected to by the laity and amounts to an uncompromising reassertion of the spiritual juris-

[8] fos. 24v–28v.   [9] 25 Henry VIII, c. 14.

diction; but it accepted that the jurisdiction rested on the King's grant and his powers as sole protector of the Church. It was certainly swimming against a strong tide, though, as we shall see, whoever devised this document did understand some things about Henry VIII.

The defenders of the Church courts had reason to rally their forces, for in 1535 Cromwell decided to look into the question. As he was advised, his planning staff had included the determination of what matters should be triable in spiritual courts among the acts they had been drafting for the past two years.[10] On July 28th, while visiting Tewkesbury, Cromwell sent instructions to his servant Richard Pollard, a barrister-at-law, in consequence of which Pollard, accompanied by others of Cromwell's servants with legal experience, met several doctors attached to the Court of Arches, among them the well known civilians Thomas Thirlby and John Oliver, themselves good King's men.[11] The discussion, which revolved around the limits of the spiritual jurisdiction, was not satisfactory. The civilians produced a set of proposals which Pollard judged to be 'in a generality and nothing in a specialty'.[12] He also thought that crimes and causes might 'rise and grow hereafter upon every of the said articles' which should be heard in secular courts, whereas so far the Church had claimed jurisdiction. It was therefore agreed that the doctors should produce a more detailed list of causes triable in Courts Christian for further discussion. Pollard's own views, however, were already settled:

> I think if it may stand with the King's grace's pleasure and yours, it were better to devise a remedy that the temporal judges may hereafter have jurisdiction of all such crimes and causes as the ecclesiastical judges have had jurisdiction heretofore, and by that means we shall have but one law within this realm, which I think better in my poor mind than to have several laws.

He would, of course, accept what the King and Cromwell resolved, but those were his opinions.

[10] *LP* ix. 725(i).
[11] SP 1/95, fo. 121 (*LP* ix. 119), Pollard to Cromwell, 18 August (1535).
[12] It is just possible that the document on Church courts just discussed was prepared for this conference, though it is not the concise 'articles' brought along by Thirlby.

Pollard's drastic solution was not adopted, nor do we know that that committee ever met again. Indeed, as is by now quite well known, the courts of the Church experienced something of a revival after the Reformation, especially in their dealings with the clergy; both their records and their activities grew more massive rather than less down to the Great Rebellion. It looks as though they owed their escape at a time when their suppression may have seemed more likely than not to the policy decision which produced Cromwell's vicegerency. This office in effect represented two things: Henry's determination to keep his Church, and his position in the Church, as nearly papal as possible, and Cromwell's desire to organize the whole Church of England under a single control. To Henry, the spiritual jurisdiction appeared as one emanation of his divinely instituted authority which he had no intention of abandoning; to that extent the memorialist who drew up the long 'edict' in his name understood the King's mind. To Cromwell, the spiritual jurisdiction was evidently less sacrosanct; he did at least consider some reduction of it, though Pollard's suggestion that it be merged totally in the temporal system was both so overwhelmingly complicated and so much counter to Henry's concept of the Church that it could not be seriously contemplated. Thus the vicegerency gave Cromwell control over what he neither could nor would abolish.

The situation was well presented in the advice Cromwell received from a member of the vicegerential office, almost certainly his deputy Dr William Petre, at the time when it was being set up.[13] Petre knew that the spiritual jurisdiction was to continue, but he advised that the Church courts – at the time he was concerned only with those of the southern province – should sit as delegates of the Crown. Cases already started, he suggested, should be ended in the King's name, and future matters should be governed by precise instructions conveyed in a royal commission to the ecclesiastical judges. He did, however, wish to redefine ecclesiastical causes. He could not understand how 'these money matters' especially of probate had got into the hands of the Church; quite correctly he pointed out that they

[13] SP 1/99, fo. 231 (*LP* ix. 1071), probably of about the middle of 1535. The mention of a commission for Cranmer may date it to late 1537 (cf. *LP* xii. II. 293), but the link is tenuous and Cranmer had to do with commissions at all sorts of times. I cannot be absolutely certain that the hand is Petre's, but it looks very much like it.

were temporal in the Roman law. Tithe, too, in practice seemed to him secular, since all disputes arising on it were over cash: 'and I would also think ecclesiastical men to be most unmeet of all other to have the handling of that thing.' Defamation and perjury 'be but brabbling and only stuff to get money for the advocates and proctors'. Thus he would restrict the Church to matrimony and divorce (since those issues were governed by the law of Scripture), and to the probate of 'small testaments' and institutions because centralizing such petty matters would be a burden to the people. The rest of his paper dealt with the office organization he wanted Cromwell to provide for the vicegerential jurisdiction.[14]

Even this degree of encroachment or reform proved too much to undertake, though this variety of opinions may help to explain why the commission for the reform of the canon law achieved nothing in the 1530's. The jurisdiction of the Church emerged untouched from the storms of the early Reformation, to trouble subsequent reformers until it evaporated in the later seventeenth century. Even that peculiarity of the English law which consigned the probate of testaments to the Church courts remained in being until 1857, though the Statute of Wills (1540) committed at least the probate of lands bequeathed by will to the common law. The Church kept its hands on movables. Despite the long-standing hostility of common lawyers and the frequent complaints, and despite some clear-cut and drastic proposals emerging from his circle of advisers, Cromwell did not take this opportunity – if opportunity it was, in view of the King's attitudes – to tackle any aspect of this problem. The courts continued as before, in some ways more so, and only the rapidly growing contempt of the laity for their strictures and fulminations obscured the fact that the grievances had had no remedy at all.

There was, however, one aspect of the spiritual jurisdiction to which Cromwell gave some attention, partly because it rendered the administration of the secular law more difficult and partly because in tackling it he was doing nothing very new. That aspect was those twin privileges of the Church, sanctuary and benefit of clergy, which offered a somewhat haphazard but also often rather inconvenient protection to criminal offenders. Both, of course, had been under attack before, and in the 1530's action

[14] For evidence that that jurisdiction operated cf. *Policy and Police*, 247–8.

involved no new reformist principle, only the completion of processes initiated years earlier. Both also have been so often discussed before this that only a few words are required here. Benefit of clergy, first attacked by statute in 1513, was so drastically reduced by successive acts exempting this or that offence from its operation that Holdsworth had the right of it when he thought the whole system was on the way out; only the reaction against Henrician severity came to preserve it in its secularized form, to act as an absurd moderator on the absurd savagery of the eighteenth-century criminal law.[15] Sanctuary posed a more troublesome problem, especially as it involved franchisal rights created by royal grant; the main attack here came in the important act of 1536 which in effect dissolved franchises (27 Henry VIII, c. 24), but that did not abolish ecclesiastical liberties with rights of sanctuary.[16] Here again earlier legislation had made a start, but it was left to Cromwell to break the back of the problem.

Cromwell thoroughly disapproved of an institution which hindered public order by protecting known criminals, and if driven to it he could override a privilege associated with the 'liberties of the Church'.[17] But he preferred to legislate it out of existence, though it would be wrong to ascribe the whole campaign to him. The first serious act, that of 1531, was certainly official and started in the Commons; he may have been behind it.[18] It imposed somewhat more realistic regulations on those taking sanctuary, but neither diminished the number of places that could grant it nor barred any offences from its operation. The next move, however, looks less likely to have come from Cromwell. When the session of early 1534 opened, the first thing to happen in the Lords was that someone unnamed made a spirited speech attacking two deficiencies in the law – sanctuaries and

---

[15] Holdsworth, *Hist. of English Law*, iii. 299–300. The act of 1532 which made prison-breaking by clerks a non-clergiable felony (23 Henry VIII, c. 11) apparently had originally a further clause which was cut off the engrossed bill. That of 1536, imposing the like penalty on servants who robbed their masters (27 Henry VIII, c. 17), originally excepted persons in major orders; this clause was crossed out, probably in the Commons.

[16] For sanctuary cf. Holdsworth, iii. 306–7; I. D. Thornley, 'The Destruction of Sanctuary,' *Tudor Studies presented to A. F. Pollard* (London 1924), 182–207.

[17] Cf. *Policy and Police*, 289–90.

[18] 22 Henry VIII, c. 14, beginning 'the King our sovereign lord, considering. . .'.

buggery, a curious pair.[19] It was put to their lordships that men committed detestable crimes but – *ut iuris periti aiunt* – escaped condign punishment: therefore it would be a good thing if any sanctuary man committing a further crime outside the sanctuary were thereafter to forfeit the privilege. Now this was precisely the point which Henry himself had made as long ago as 1519, in a conference over the claims of the Westminster sanctuary, and it seems perfectly possible that this move in the Lords was directly inspired by him.[20] The House ordered the judges to prepare a bill, but nothing came of all this for the time being. However, Cromwell maintained his interest and on the eve of the last session of the Reformation Parliament resolved 'specially to speak' to the King 'of utter destruction of sanctuaries'.[21] He wished simply, and wisely, to abolish the whole system, but once again this was more than Henry could stomach, anxious as always to preserve ecclesiastical claims once they were declared to be derived from him; and Cromwell could only get an act which did something more towards strict control of sanctuary men inside their refuge.[22]

Yet sanctuary was one issue over which Cromwell did not give up. He tried again in 1540, planning an act for the 'determination of sanctuaries', and this time he did obtain a formidable and much more general statute.[23] The preamble recalled Henry's earlier view that sanctuary men should not be able to commit further crimes with impunity, and the act then abolished all rights of sanctuary except in churches and churchyards (where the right was anyway limited to forty days). The preamble of the act as passed also recognized that the total abolition of all forms of refuge was undesirable: such places were needed 'in every commonwealth by the law of mercy for some causes and offences'. The act therefore created eight new sanctuaries in named towns spread over the realm in which men could take refuge for all but major crimes.[24] In this way sanctuary became a purely secular, statutory and administrative business. However, it is not clear whether this modification of the intended abolition

---

[19] *LJ* i. 59b. For buggery see below, p. 148.
[20] Thornley, *Tudor Studies*, 201.   [21] *LP* x. 254.
[22] 27 Henry VIII, c. 19.   [23] *LP* xv. 438; 32 Henry VIII, c. 12.
[24] Murder, rape, burglary, robbery, arson, sacrilege. Treason had already been removed from protection by 24 Henry VIII, c. 13. For the refuge towns see Thornley, *Tudor Studies*, 204 n.1.

was part of the government's plans: it looks as though the original bill was modified in Parliament. It was introduced in the Lords before Cromwell's fall and quickly passed; in the Commons it met sufficient opposition to be replaced by a new bill not sent up again until the last day of the session when the Lords read it three times and passed it.[25] It could have been this opposition that produced the concession of sanctuary towns: nothing else in the act explains the substitution of a new bill, and the system worked pretty badly, which indicates a certain probability of unofficial devising. A slip attached to the Original Act stresses that 'the Lords declared their mind concerning Wells – that the same is Wells in Somerset', which is to say that no one meant to create a sanctuary in the small Norfolk town of Wells-next-the-sea; this supports the interpretation that no list of sanctuary towns, and therefore no provision for them at all, had been in the government bill which the Lords sent down to the Commons. Cromwell had gone between the passage of the first bill and the production of the second; the man who simply wanted to end sanctuaries would hardly have planned to bring the principle back in another guise. Though he achieved a good deal, his out-and-out opposition to the whole concept seems to have suffered defeat at the hands first of the King and then of the Commons.

For the rest, Cromwell and his reforms did not touch the law and jurisdiction of the Church. In the law secular the story runs very differently. The deficiencies of common lawyers – their greed, the law's delays and uncertainties, the dangers of corruption – had excited criticism for quite as long as the better advertised shortcomings of the Church courts. It is true that Cromwell was himself a common lawyer and that the King's service was full of men trained in that school, but only ignorant prejudice would suppose that common lawyers always form a unanimous phalanx to preserve their way of life and its abuses. At all times there have been some at least who wished to reform the law rather than embalm it. Three well-known critics in Cromwell's circle expressed themselves on the subject. Starkey, speaking through the mouth of his fictional Reginald Pole, roundly attacked the whole English system of law, making the usual complaints and proposing that the law be reduced to a knowable code, or better still that it be replaced by the more systematic civil law.

[25] *LJ* i. 141a–b, 142a, 143a, 160b.

Richard Morison, possibly inspired by this, also expressed the common feelings about lawyers' sordid habits and their use of bad French and worse Latin; he even tried his hand at codifying the land law, a task which understandably defeated one who seems never to have heard of Lyttelton's *Tenures*.[26] Neither of these close associates of Cromwell's was a common lawyer, but John Rastell, that migrant from the More circle, certainly was. And Rastell felt quite as certain that sweeping reforms were required. Of the five bills he wanted Cromwell to promote in Parliament, three touched law reform and all were substantial: one 'for the reformation of the pleading in the common law' (perhaps to replace French by English), a second to reform the Court of Chancery especially with respect to its use of injunctions and witnesses, and a third to reduce the excessive fees taken in all the courts of the realm.[27] An obscure proposal that by Act of Parliament £10,000 be taken from 'the men of the long robe' and transferred to those 'of the short robe', which also came from Cromwell's staff, certainly manifested hostility to lawyers, whatever may have been precisely intended.[28]

Thus the advice offered to Cromwell circled around very fundamental reform, and some of the schemes to appear were grandiose. In particular those schemers designed new courts with something resembling abandon. The poor law draft, as we have seen, originally provided for a council or court with large judicial as well as administrative powers, and there was a plan for a council-court to administer the heresy laws.[29] An even more extravagant proposal was that which created a standing army financed out of surpluses achieved by putting all bishops and all remaining monasteries on an annual stipend of 1000 marks. The scheme was very much concerned with a puritanical reform in religious houses and a proper residential use of secularized lands – it has a commonwealth air, all right – but its main and most original notions touched the use of the money for the purposes of defence. In all this one may hear, with some difficulty, echoes of Starkey's advice to Henry to use the new properties for the better education of the young both in learning and in martial skills, but the proposal, cast in the form of a draft bill, went very

[26] Cf. *Proc. Brit. Acad.* liv (1968), 176–80.
[27] SP 1/85, fo. 100 (*LP* vii. 1043).
[28] *LP* ix. 725(i).   [29] Above, pp. 72–3.

much further. It certainly reached Cromwell, one of whose filing clerks endorsed it, and may well have originated in his circle; quite certainly he never showed any further interest in it.[30] The man behind this plan also believed in setting up new courts: he invented a Court of Centeners, resident at Coventry, which was both to administer the organization of the army and to adjudicate 'all causes between the suitors thereunto', those suitors being mainly 'the men of war'. Its judges were the lord admiral and someone called 'the provost' (the commander-in-chief); there was to be a treasurer with particular receivers in every shire; the draft says quite a bit about the rendering and auditing of accounts. But it has no word about the organization of the court as a court, a fact which raises the suspicion that the inventor of the scheme was no lawyer; the other man who looked over the plan and noted queries in the margin had cause to scribble the question, 'de aliis officiis ad eandem curiam pertinentibus'. This is just one of the several signs that this pipedream represents no considered or central part of a general programme, though, of course, the fact that such revolutionary ideas could be entertained remains interesting. There were Utopian doodlers among the people who looked to Cromwell.

More specifically concerned with law reform was yet another project involving the creation of a court, the Court of Justices or Conservators of the Common Weal, a project also cast in the form of a draft statute.[31] Even more than the Centeners' draft it is manifestly the work of a commonwealth man: one need only look at the preamble with its reference to good statutes 'for the augmentation, maintenance and good increase of the common weal of this his realm'. This plan tried to solve the notorious problem of enforcing statutes penal or popular, acts made for the control of the economy and for social welfare. What was the use of those acts when they were regularly ignored with impunity? In place of the admittedly inefficient enforcement of the acts by

---

[30] BM, Cleo. E. iv, fos. 214–20 (*LP* xiv. I. 871). The *LP* dating, 1539, is too late: the draft assumes the continued existence of all monasteries except those dissolved in 1536 and was very likely composed in the summer of that year. The scheme is discussed by L. Stone, 'The Political Programme of Thomas Cromwell,' *Bull. Inst. Hist. Res.* xxiv (1951), 1–18, and by myself, ibid. xxv (1952), 126–30.

[31] Printed by T. F. T. Plucknett, 'Some Proposed Legislation of Henry VIII,' *Trans. Royal Hist. Soc.* 1936, 119–44; and cf. my remarks in *Bull. Inst. Hist. Res.* xxv (1952), 123–4.

informer action in Exchequer or Common Pleas, the draft proposed a special court with powers to create a detective force
throughout the realm (serjeants or servants of the common weal).
It is rather more careful to work out the details of organization
and the process to be used; it specifies that the course of the
common law be employed and regulates the relations of the
Conservators with sheriffs and escheators. Its most dangerous
clause in effect equips the Conservators with power to create
offences at will if some action 'in and upon the land as in or upon
any waters fresh or salt' seems to them contrary to the interests
of the common weal. In fact, the draft embodies at its most complete the passion for social engineering which lay behind so much
humanist thought on the welfare of mankind. Plucknett was
rather more impressed than I can be by the evidence that the
author was 'a philosophical jurist as well as a practising lawyer':
in the light of all the other schemes floating about, this one is not
extraordinary though it is striking. But what is striking belongs to
the realm of philosophy, not of law, and I doubt very much
whether the mind that conceived it was that of a practising
lawyer. Cromwell ignored it, too.

Above all, one must be struck by the difference between these
proposals for new courts and the new courts that were actually
set up. Court-making was an industry in the early sixteenth
century, and Cromwell, in particular, believed in adding in this
way to the effectiveness of law and justice in the realm. There
are good reasons for thinking that both the Courts of Star Chamber and Requests received their settled form during his ascendancy, and though before the nineteenth century neither he nor
anyone else ever cleansed the stables of Chancery he did provide
even that court with a measure of organized efficiency.[32] Above
all, he was responsible for the creation of the Courts of Augmentations and Wards, models followed soon after his fall by the
Courts of General Surveyors and of First Fruits and Tenths, even
as they themselves were modelled somewhat on the Court of
Duchy Chamber. Even a quick glance at the statutes setting up
these courts, with their masses of necessary technical detail, will
show how far from ready for action were the schemes for
Centeners and Conservators; even the Council to Avoid

[32] W. J. Jones, *The Elizabethan Court of Chancery* (Oxford, 1967), 8, 50–1,
164.

Vagabonds, though apparently Cromwell let it go forward to Parliament, would have needed a great deal of additional working out, if we are to go by the extant draft.

Augmentations and Wards owed their organization to expert lawyers, probably in the main to Lord Chancellor Audley, Cromwell's most trusted legal adviser, but they exemplify Cromwell's own double concern: the improvement of government machinery, and the provision of more and better justice. These courts, more than those dreamt of but not proceeded with, could do a great deal to meet one standard complaint, namely that the mass of suitors had caused a major pile-up in the regular courts of the realm. Whether these reforms achieved anything is not at present known; we need much more investigation of the law and its administration before we can venture upon a guess. But I will record my conviction that one of Cromwell's reforming purposes touched the need to provide better and swifter justice for those who came seeking it. Stephen Vaughan, it will be remembered, knew well how much of Cromwell's time was spent on every man's plaints and on endeavours to satisfy the demands for justice; and he usefully emphasized that Cromwell was quite exceptionally active in attending to this normal part of any king's councillor's work.[33] Such ambitions underlay his reforms in the Chancery, and in part they underlay the creation of financial courts. He planned to do more. In 1532, a bill concerning Chancery and Exchequer received one reading in the Commons; its contents are unknown and it was not reintroduced, but it is most likely to have dealt with the abuses in fees and speed which burdened the subject.[34] More specifically, in late 1533 Cromwell planned an amending act for the so-called Star Chamber Acts which would have empowered the lord chancellor and two judges to sit despite the absence of other officers demanded by the statutes: this was to be 'for speed of justice to the King's subjects'.[35] Like the majority of ideas jotted down in that paper, this one came to nothing, but it shows the constant purpose.

Better justice is one end of law reform; better law another. In the history of law reform, which is both halting and continuous, the 1530's provide a rather purposeful interlude. With respect to the criminal law I have already discussed the central problem

[33] Above, p. 45.   [34] *LP* vi. 120(1).
[35] BM, Titus B. i, fo. 161 (*LP* vi. 1381).

of supposedly ecclesiastical privilege, and for the rest I will refer myself to Holdsworth's summary which shows that in the Cromwell era an existing reforming policy continued unchecked and not much augmented, though the measures of that decade always tend to cut through the thickets more forcefully and successfully than had been usual before.[36] The work done in the civil law and in controlling lawyers' malpractices is more significant. The old law, as is well known, was really built around one central theme, that of real property, and under Cromwell the law governing this underwent a major revolution. Between them, the Statute of Uses of 1536 and the Statute of Wills of 1540 transformed the principles of landownership by vesting the legal estate in all land in the beneficiary of the issues and by legalizing the bequeathing by will of two-thirds of all land held in knight's service as well as of all property held in socage. However swiftly and drastically the intentions of these two acts were modified by lawyers' devices (assisted at times by the usual inadequate drafting of all law-reform statutes), the fact remains that from 1540 onwards the law concerning possession of land rested fundamentally on this new legislation.[37] The making of these two acts has been so thoroughly and so recently discussed that I need not go over it again.[38] Dr Ives suggested that the Statute of Uses may have owed its stringent and impracticable aspects to Henry VIII, while the necessary modification of its least sensible provisions in the Statute of Wills reflects, he thinks, Cromwell's attitudes.

This may well have been so. Certainly both acts had a difficult history. The problem of uses and primer seisin recurs among Cromwell's papers but never in connection with plans of his own: he inherited the unfinished bills of 1531 and 1532, and was instructed to prepare the latter, but that is all.[39] In 1535, the notes prepared by his staff mention wards and primer seisin, a linking of themes which looks forward to the legislation of 1540 rather than that of 1536.[40] As for the Statute of Wills, that can indeed be

---

[36] Holdsworth, *Hist. of English Law*, iv. 501–32.

[37] Cf. A. W. B. Simpson, *An Introduction to the History of the Land Law* (Oxford, 1961), 173–86.

[38] E. W. Ives, 'The Genesis of the Statute of Uses,' *Eng. Hist. Rev.* lxxxii (1967), 673–97.   [39] *LP* iv. 6043(3); v. 394; vi. 120(1).

[40] *LP* ix. 725(ii). The Statute of Wills reserved the feudal rights of the Crown (especially wardship) of which there is no express mention in the Statute of Uses; while 1540, of course, also saw the setting up of the Court of Wards.

tentatively linked with Cromwell. It was originally planned for
1539. On the eve of the session Cromwell sent a reminder to
Henry to get the judges going on certain problems: one of them
read, 'the wards of your tenants be taken away by wills'.[41] At this
point, therefore, it seems that the interests of lesser lords were to
the fore, or at least were posing the legal problem, which may
account for the fate of the bill. It was introduced by the lord
chancellor in the Lords, which makes it fully official; the House
after reading it once, suspiciously committed it to the lord chief
justice for revision; after a second reading, a week later, it
lapsed.[42] Perhaps it was redrafted; at any rate, in the next session
it passed without difficulty.[43] Section 4 of the act still contained
the point that Cromwell had raised in 1539.

Cromwell's close connection with these important reforms in
the land law emerges even more clearly from the concomitant
attempts to do something about the notorious problem of uncertain title, a very ancient grievance. The difficulties were
created by the secretive ways of conveyancers, in consequence of
which both legitimate ambiguity and downright fraud beset the
establishing of rights in property. One obvious solution was to
arrange for the proper and public registration of all transactions,
and in 1533 or 1534 someone, probably Rastell, submitted a
relevant scheme to Cromwell.[44] This took the form of the creation,
by letters patent, of an office for the making of all conveyances by
deeds and indentures, as well as other similar instruments, in
London and Southwark, with no one else permitted to draft these
profitable documents. There was a suggestion that the scheme
might later be extended throughout the realm. The reform justi-

---

[41] SP 1/158, fo. 159 (*LP* xv. 439). The *LP* date, 1540, presumably derives
from the date of the statute, but *LP* were not aware of the earlier attempt.
Another note in the same paper reads 'for Giles Heron's matter for his
offence'; though not attainted until 1540, after a good deal of discussion
how best to proceed with him, Heron was arrested in February 1539
(*LP* xiv. I. 358).

[42] *LJ* i. 114a, 115b.

[43] Ibid. 154a, 157a. That the bill was not introduced until after Cromwell's
fall proves nothing in view of his earlier attempt.

[44] SP 2/O, fos. 346–8 (*LP* vi. 1615). It is endorsed 'for Rastell and Martin
Pyrry', two people also associated on another occasion (*LP* vi. 1176, 1457).
The draft is in the form of an English letter to the civic officers of
London and not at all in the proper Latin form (*omnibus ad quos
presentes littere pervenerint...*) of correct letters patent granting the
office to nominees, as the superscription suggests.

fied itself on the grounds that forgeries were producing conflict and uncertainty, so that the Council were overwhelmed with needless arbitrations. The officers were to hold for life, to employ clerks, to earn stated fees, and to keep a register of all documents drawn by them.[45] Rather obviously, Rastell was seeking the sort of monopoly patent which became familiar later in the century, under the guise of serving the common weal; rather significantly, his approach failed.

The general idea, however, was not forgotten. At one point, Cromwell's drafters played about with some pretty odd notions. Among the reforms of the land law which were current at the time was the abolition of entail below the ranks of the nobility; a bill projected for that purpose included provisions for all uses to be enrolled in Commons Pleas and for all deeds of conveyance to be read out from the pulpits of parish churches, after which they were to be ratified by the vicar's signature and registered in the shire town.[46] This barely worked-out mixture of sound purpose and silly devices was filed away, but late in 1535 Cromwell's planners received instructions to prepare a real bill, a very much more remarkable document. This was a plan for a full-scale system of land-registration.[47] In words which partially recall the phrases of Rastell's draft patent, the preamble pleaded 'the great strifes, debates and variances' constantly occurring from uncertainty of title, which uncertainty arose out of fraudulent conveyancing and unwritten agreements. It goes on to disallow all conveyances to uses or trusts unless made by sealed deeds and enrolled, and orders all the enrolment of all other 'evidences and

[45] Deeds, indentures, obligations, last wills and testaments, letters of attorney, depositions of witnesses.

[46] SP 1/56, fos. 36–9 (*LP* iv. 6043[6]), printed Holdsworth, *Hist. of English Law*, iv. 572–4. This is the bill which Holdsworth thought was one side of a bargain between Henry, seeking feudal rights, and a nobility reluctant to part with enfeoffment to uses (ibid. 450–3). As Ives has shown, no such bargain was ever in hand, and the bill is a piece of ill-conceived private enterprise of uncertain date (*Eng. Hist. Rev.* lxxii [1967], 677–80). I would place it somewhere around 1533–4; it might be linked with Rastell.

[47] SP 1/101, fos. 303–21 (*LP* x. 246[6]); printed Holdsworth, iv. 582–6, and briefly discussed by Lehmberg, *Reformation Parliament*, 238. The bill was to come into effect on 1 August 1536, which is also the date appointed by the act as passed. This bill takes the form of a set of articles preceded by a preamble and general enacting clause, a form found elsewhere in Cromwell's legislation which probably reflects an earlier intention to proceed by administrative ordinance.

writings' touching 'lands, tenements and hereditaments'. There was to be a master of enrolments appointed by letters patent in every shire, as well as a clerk of enrolments to serve him at the appointment of the lord chancellor. They were to have a seal of their office, and every transaction submitted to them was to be sealed by them within forty days, unless within six months it had been registered in Chancery, King's Bench, Common Pleas or Exchequer. Deeds not so enrolled were declared void. Careful regulations dealt with registration and search fees, and prevented fraud or undue delay on the part of masters and clerks. The serious purpose of the draft is underlined by six provisos saving the established rights of municipal officers (who did some enrolling of deeds),[48] of manorial courts where copyhold deeds were habitually registered, and the practices of the central courts;[49] the problem of land lying in more than one shire was not forgotten. Lastly, obligations and other documents concerning 'personal things' might also be presented for enrolment, but this was to be at the pleasure of the parties; failure to enrol them did not invalidate them. In this last provision there is again an echo of Rastell's draft patent, but it should be noted that the bill avoided the worst feature of that intended monopoly by confining itself to registration: the actual drafting of deeds would continue in the hands of the people who were already making a living at it.

Nevertheless, the scheme did in a manner derive from Rastell's plan. The details are very much more carefully worked out, and that list of provisos indicates that everything had been done to produce a bill ready for introduction into Parliament. Was it introduced? There is no such act on the book; instead we have the very short Statute of Enrolments of 1536.[50] Lacking a preamble, it briefly enacts that all transactions by bargain and sale were to pass by sealed indentures enrolled within six months either in the central courts at Westminster or before at least one justice of the peace and the clerk of the peace in the counties. There is one proviso saving the powers of town authorities, no

---

[48] Cf. G. H. Martin, 'The Registration of Deeds of Title in the Medieval Borough,' *Essays. . .Kathleen Major*, 151–73.

[49] Especially, of course, the final concords of Common Pleas, the most popular form of registering deeds, characteristically by means of a fictitious and collusive action at law.

[50] 27 Henry VIII, c. 16. That this took the place of the draft is shown by the fact that both were intended to come into effect on the same day.

more. By comparison with the draft, the act confined registration to bargains and sales, which left out many other forms of conveyance, and abandoned the whole new machinery of enrolment. There are some curious features about the Original Act. The bill was first passed in the Commons, and the engrossment is in a hand that wrote no others, an individual hand and not one of the usual court hands that drew parchment bills. The same hand added a proviso on the bill for the decay of houses, and it therefore seems a reasonable conjecture that it was the hand of the clerk of the House, Robert Urmeston or Armstrong. The total absence of any preamble, by this time very unusual especially in government bills, taken together with that swift running hand, rather casually written, strongly suggests that we have here the result of some kind of emergency. If the government had introduced its comprehensive land-register bill but could not get it through the House, and if it was then decided to save what could be saved by producing, possibly in committee, a bill covering a bit of the ground in acceptable terms, the extant act might well have looked as in fact it does.

One can in this case do no more than conjecture, but I suggest that this reconstruction seems probable and takes account of all the available evidence. If I am right, Cromwell tried for an act which would certainly have been a major reform in the law and of enormous benefit to honest dealings in land, but it offended two powerful interests. Landowners, who as purchasers might welcome publicity, were less well inclined to it as vendors, while conveyancers have always resented anything that subjects their operations to the general scrutiny. The suspicion of a proper registration for dealings in land is so strong in the common-law mind that to this day we do not possess the land-register planned by Thomas Cromwell. At the time it may well have been argued that the inclusion of uses was doubtful at a moment when the whole practice was under fundamental review, but it need not be doubted that entrenched interests simply proved too strong. The government did well enough in the circumstances when they secured the concession of the statute as passed, though a main part of transactions in land now escaped the net and the county registration scheme without specialist officers never really worked.

The Statutes of Uses, Wills and Enrolment were the major

achievements of law reform in the 1530's, but by no means the only ones. Plenty of relevant acts were passed in those nine sessions, but on a closer look an interesting pattern emerges. The relatively few acts of the Reformation Parliament, at least before its last session, nearly all concerned law-enforcement: acts against the standard methods for evading the consequences of crime. They include the measures limiting sanctuary and benefit of clergy; the act which ended the practice of pleading that an offence was properly triable in another county or a liberty; the act reorganizing the gaols throughout the realm; the reenactment (with improvements) of Henry VII's statute against false jury verdicts; and the act subjecting pirates to the common law.[51] Important enough in their comprehensive attack on lawlessness, these statutes look certain to be of government provenance, and nearly all were first introduced in the Commons. Acts which attended to other matters of the law were three. An unofficial act started in the Commons abolished felonious forfeitures for killers of thieves caught in the act; this has very much the air of a private member's bill. The Sodomy Act of 1534 is curious. As we saw, the person who opened the subject of sanctuary in 1534 added that it was equally deplorable to find that the terrible offence of unnatural crime carried no penalty in the law, and the judges were instructed to prepare bills on both subjects.[52] They did nothing about sanctuary, perhaps because the Commons were engaged on a bill, but the buggery bill was quickly presented and passed.[53] If, as I suggested, the King lurked behind the move on one subject he may also have been responsible for the other: the mixture of prudery and ferocity in his character fits the situation. The only law reform of this period which has the appearance of commonwealth and Cromwell about it is the act of 1532 which regulated the declaration of so-called statutes staple, the most

---

[51] 22 Henry VIII, cc. 2, 14; 23 Henry VIII, cc. 1, 2, 3, 11; 25 Henry VIII, c. 3; 27 Henry VIII, c. 4. The Piracy Act was forecast in Cromwell's notes (*LP* x. 254). Although not limited in duration, it was once more enacted in the following session (28 Henry VIII, c. 15), apparently so that the word 'traitors' could be included in the description of pirates. This is the only change in wording.

[52] Above, pp. 136–7.

[53] *LJ* i. 60a–b, 61b, 65b. There is a curious correction in the parchment bill: the whole crucial description of the crime – 'vice of buggery committed with mankind or beast' – is written over an erasure.

commonly used recognisance for debt.[54] The bill had a careful
preamble explaining the legal problem; it spoke as if in the
King's name; but the Original Act is in a distinctly unofficial
hand, and the bill started in the Commons. Still, even if the
initiative was private it is not improper to suspect a commonwealth move here.

On the other hand, there had already been some isolated
attempts to deal with more definitely legal reforms. A bill concerning recoveries to uses (the possible abuse of a legal fiction)
failed in 1531, and one for bankruptcy got as far as a second
reading in the Commons in 1532.[55] The first submerged in the
general legislation for uses, while the second waited till 1543 to
become law.[56] For the first session of 1534, Cromwell contemplated the problem of the King's rights as affected by the granting of reversions of offices and gifts; he also mulled over the
possibility of resuming all joint patents and patents of offices
in Wales held by Welshmen.[57] These ideas mixed legal reform
with a tightening up of the King's hold on the realm and its
government – and the royal finances. Of the ten bills that failed
in that session, none concerned law reform, unless one were to
include one which would have prevented aliens from keeping
inns.[58] Thus down to the session of 27 Henry VIII, law reform
played a very small part in the thinking of government and the
work of Parliament, except that the administration of the criminal
law was overhauled in line with long-established policy. In that
last session of the Reformation Parliament, however, Cromwell
began to turn his attention seriously to the law. Not only did he
obtain the reform of the land law; he also planned something
concerning the rights of orphans in London, he wanted a law
against excessive interest on loans, he hinted at a criticism of the
Court of Common Pleas, and for the first time he gave evidence
that he shared the general feeling against lawyers' malpractices
in a note forecasting the reduction of the number of attorneys in
the shires, 'which persons', he added, 'be the cause of great plea
and dissension'.[59] Perhaps he had read Starkey; and he certainly

---

[54] 23 Henry VIII, c. 6.   [55] *LP* iv. 6043(3); vi. 120(1).
[56] 34 & 35 Henry VIII, c. 4.   [57] *LP* vi. 1381.
[58] These ten bills appear in *LJ* for 25 Henry VIII; they are all concerned
with trade and industry.
[59] *LP* x. 254.

had decided to adopt the advice of his planners who a little earlier had recommended action to restrain 'the abuses of lawyers' and against usury.[60] In passing we may note that the precise measure against usury – limiting interest to 10% – which Cromwell included in his plans became law in 1546.[61]

Thus by 1536 the matter of the common weal had come for Cromwell to include the shortcomings of the law. The emergency Parliament of that year offered no opportunity to tackle the problem: the new Succession Act and the disposal of the Boleyn faction were business enough at such short notice. Even so, the solicitor general introduced a bill for increasing the fines on delinquent juries, a trailer from the earlier policy, and Cromwell did get his orphans bill through the Commons, only to see it rejected in the Lords.[62] A bill for the manumission of bondmen, which the Lords read three times before throwing it out, may well have been of unofficial promotion; no doubt it failed because it still affected the rights of manorial lords.[63] The programme for legal reform therefore devolved upon Cromwell's last Parliament, and this time he tackled it with his accustomed energy and planned determination, sweeping matters both great and small into his net.

The campaign began with a petition allegedly from the commons of England (not the House of Commons) to the King and Lords of his Parliament. The surviving draft was among Cromwell's papers; whether he had it prepared cannot be determined, but evidently he was familiar with it, and the outcome suggests that he used it.[64] The petitioners complained bitterly of the 'learned men in the laws' who 'for their own singular lucre, avail and profit' promoted disputes among the people and used their skills to advance fraud and hinder the truth. All this and high fees troubled especially men of little substance. The com-

---

[60] LP ix. 725(ii).   [61] 37 Henry VIII, c. 9.

[62] LJ i. 89b, 98a, 99b.

[63] Ibid. 99a; cf. A. Savine, 'Bondmen under the Tudors,' Trans. Royal Hist. Soc. 1903, 235–89.

[64] SP 2/Q, fos. 208–10 (LP vii. 1611[3]). The date must be conjectural, but since the events of 1539–40 can be seen in measure to flow from this petition I would reject LP's 1534 and opt for 1539. The draft is 'properly' set out on large sheets, as was customary in Cromwell's office, but it is not in a clerk's hand. The hand is quite similar to that which drafted Rastell's petition for a patent (above, p. 144), but certain differences, especially in the capitals, make me hesitate to identify the two.

plaints read curiously like the earlier ones about spiritual courts. There was corruption both among lawyers themselves and among sheriffs and their deputies – writs could not be executed without bribes. It was useless, the petition went on, to appeal to the House of Commons, 'for that so many learned men be rulers in your Common House', and it therefore begged the King to get the Lords and judges to devise remedial measures. This was an important point: petitions to Parliament were usually channelled through the Commons, and a case had to be made for asking for legislative initiative from the Lords. The petitioners especially wanted laws to speed up justice and establish fixed scales of fees, but the general tenor is wider. Finally they revealed their intellectual origins by hoping that in this way 'a universal common and public weal' might be created.

Thus it was recognized that law reform would have to start in the Lords if it was to overcome the lawyers' opposition in the Commons. For the 1539 session, Cromwell's own known plans included only a bill to limit the period of ancient prescription,[65] a measure adumbrated in the petition, and those months spent in the battles over proclamations and six articles did indeed prove largely barren. A minor reform clarifying the rights of joint tenants and tenants in common looks to have been a private promotion; it was so poorly drafted that it had to be amended only a year later by what was possibly an official bill to include tenants for life or term of years.[66] The act which by freeing the ex-religious from legal disabilities signalled the end of any attempt to preserve vestiges of monasticism, though official, ran into difficulties. Introduced in the Lords by the solicitor general, it passed there readily enough; the Commons replaced the government's bill with one of their own which the Lords accepted after getting the lord chancellor to review it.[67] The act as passed lacks a preamble (in the manner of the Enrolment Act); it is very brief and grudging; one may conjecture a more generous official intention blocked by the legal interest which feared the intrusion of yet another body of men into the complications of inheritance. And the act altering the custom of gavelkind for the benefit of

[65] LP xiv. I. 655.
[66] 31 Henry VIII, c. 1, introduced in the Commons; the original act is in a very unofficial hand. 32 Henry VIII, c. 32, also started in the Commons, has a certain official air to it. One cannot be sure.
[67] 31 Henry VIII, c. 6; LJ i. 105b, 106b, 121a, 122a, 125b.

thirty-four named landowners from Kent, though official enough,[68] formed no part of law reform proper; it was really in effect a multiple private act presumably initiated by the first beneficiary named – Thomas Lord Cromwell who had lately acquired property in the shire.

That the real campaign for law reform had started is neverthe-less proved by the bills that failed. Two started in the Commons; one of them, trying to secure overseas debts, seems to have been too sectional to please the Lords who rejected it, while another, which attempted to deal with a genuine grievance (the defeating of justice by exploiting technical errors in pleading) was lost for lack of time.[69] This second one was revived and passed in the following session. Four bills, however, definitely emanated from the government and followed the urging of the petitioners to see reform initiated in the Lords. Lord Chancellor Audley introduced a bill for wills, one for the abolition (probably shortening) of Trinity term, and the one for the limitation of prescription which Cromwell had planned.[70] The first two lapsed for the moment, while the last one was rejected for reasons unknown; all three came back next year. And Chief Justice Edward Montague had yet another go at legislating for the misbehaviour of jurors; after reluctantly giving his bill a first reading quite early in the session, the Lords managed to forget it.[71] Corrupt juries had their friends in high places, for good reason.

Thus law reform became the issue of Cromwell's last parlia-mentary session. His notes show that he was now going all out for it: 'an act to be devised for devices contrary to divers statutes made by learned men' is not likely to mean only the Statute of Wills (devising), but rather to reflect a general assault on legal trickery.[72] At any rate, law reform was in the air. The keynote was set by Cromwell's voice in matters legal, the lord chancellor. On the second day of the session, Audley presented to the Lords what the clerk called a *Liber Memorialis* in which he outlined seven reforms that he thought necessary.[73] When a man enfeoffed

---

[68] 31 Henry VIII, c. 3; introduced in the Lords by the attorney general (*LJ* i. 107b), it was drawn in the form of a royal ordinance.

[69] *LJ* i. 112b, 114b.

[70] *LJ* i. 114a, 115b; 119b (this sole entry speaks of abolition but, to judge from the later act, was probably in error); 114a, 115a.

[71] Ibid. 107b, 110b.

[72] *LP* xv. 438.   [73] *LJ* i. 130a.

another out of his wife's jointure and without her consent, this was to be without prejudice to the wife and her heirs. Leases made to tenants in tail were to be held good. Unjust disseisin was to create no lawful descent of lands. Protection was to be offered to any who revealed murders or felonies committed by several persons; presumably he had in mind participants in crime willing to save their necks. Marriages of minors without the consent of parents or guardians were to be prevented. Once again, the government tried for a law increasing the penalties for false jury verdicts and perjury. And a law was required concerning distraint: perhaps to abolish the very burdensome process of distress infinite which could beggar a man innocently involved in another's legal troubles.[74]

Not that the results of Audley's move came up to intentions. Only one of the proposals passed simply into law; the act which declared wrongful disseisin to be no bar to recovery unless the disseisor had remained in peaceful possession for five years.[75] Even in this case it sounds as though Parliament weakened the lord chancellor's original point. The first two items in the memorial were amalgamated into an act which protected the rights of lessees and included a clause exactly embodying Audley's idea for protecting wives.[76] This had no easy passage: started in the Lords and passed there after revision by the chief justice of Common Pleas, it was replaced by another bill in the Commons which the Lords accepted.[77] We cannot now tell what the Commons disliked in the original proposal, but they may have removed the special case of tenants in tail of whom there is no trace in the act. A bill against the marriages of minors easily passed the Lords, only to vanish in the Commons. The remaining points never even got under way; once again juries escaped, and no one seemed sufficiently keen to make it a happy life for people who turned king's evidence.

However, the government programme was not confined to Audley's memorial. The Statute of Wills now went through, as did the act limiting rights created by prescription to sixty years

---

[74] Cf. Marjorie Blatcher, 'Distress Infinite and the Contumacious Sheriff,' *Bull. Inst. Hist. Res.* xiii (1935–6), 146–50.

[75] 32 Henry VIII, c. 33, a Lords' bill which encountered no difficulties.

[76] 32 Henry VIII, c. 28.

[77] *LJ* i. 131a, 136a–b, is not very clear on the history of the bill; the Original Act started in the Commons.

for titles resting on writs of right and fifty years for those arising upon a possessory assize.[78] This was the act which Cromwell had planned in 1539 and which had then failed in the Lords. It was again presented in the Upper House, passed without difficulty, and received only three sensible amendments in the Commons to protect the rights of persons who might quite inadvertently be affected by this change in the law.[79] Another left-over from the previous session, the act limiting the length of Trinity term, started as an official bill in the Lords and went through after a slight revision.[80] So did the act against the abuse of mispleading which had been privately promoted the previous year. Its history now is obscure: the most likely reconstruction is that it again started in the Commons and was by the Lords committed to the lord chief justice; that then the Lower House sent up an additional clause against the negligence of attorneys in the Westminster courts; and that because of this irregularity the Lords returned bill and billet once more to the Commons.[81] The billet is really very odd. It has nothing to do with the body of the bill which it in no way qualifies, and it therefore looks as though anti-lawyer agitation in the Commons succeeded (despite all those lawyers there) in tacking a second grievance to the first, to ease these matters through. If this is right, the bill was no government measure. The Commons also initiated an act which protected debtors who had claims on the estate of a person deceased; this was an unofficial bill.[82] The same is true of its counterpart which enabled executors to recover debts owed to testators.[83] The act against collusive recoveries suffered by tenants for life (uses and entailed estate) whereby the reversioners lost their rights, which also started in the Lower House, could on the face of it have been either official or not; since very likely it derived from the old bill first promoted in 1531, private initiative seems

---

[78] 32 Henry VIII, cc. 1, 2.
[79] *LJ* i. 142b, 143a, 148a.
[80] 32 Henry VIII, c. 21; *LJ* i. 131a, 141b, 142a, 144b.
[81] 32 Henry VIII, c. 30. The Original Act started in the Commons and so did the proviso which is in a different hand. On the other hand, *LJ* i. 138a–b, 139a, 140b, would suggest that both originated in the Lords. There is no suggestion that the Commons replaced a Lords' bill, and in this conflict of evidence the Original Act must weigh more heavily than the often deficient Journal.
[82] 32 Henry VIII, c. 5.
[83] 32 Henry VIII, c. 38.

more probable.[84] On the other hand, the important Statute of Fines, which remedied a serious deficiency in the law by confirming that fines levied in Common Pleas bound also tenants in tail, was certainly a government measure, even though it started in the Commons: it clearly said so, and we know that Cromwell personally interested himself in the bill.[85] It was the Lords who first saw the act which marked yet another step away from the absurdities of late-medieval canon law by confining bars to marriage to genuine precontracts only and to those prohibited degrees that could be found expressly stated in Scripture.[86]

All these acts were useful in improving the administration of the law and in easing the difficulties of the subject, and in them official initiative in the Lords had clearly some support from private initiative in the Commons. The measure designed to tackle the real grievances of those petitioners of 1539 ran into much more serious difficulties. Early in the session, the Lords received a bill to punish certain malpractices by which good rights were lost – corruption of juries and the buying of false titles. They read it a first time and committed it to the master of the rolls. After two more readings it was recommitted, we do not know to whom, and after yet another reading was handed to the chief justice of Common Pleas for final polishing. Thereafter it passed the House, evidently after a good deal of resistance. Nevertheless it failed to please the Commons who substituted a new bill. To this the Lords assented, though not without further weakening it by limiting actions upon the statute to within one year from the alleged offence.[87] The act as passed is quite brief and pointless; it adds almost nothing to the existing legislation against maintenance and embracery which it confirms. One can hardly credit that the bill hammered out so laboriously in the Lords and rejected in the Commons was as short and meaningless as that. Rather it looks very much as though the major attempt to restrain the legal profession from notorious misbehaviour (Cromwell's 'devices contrary to divers statutes') was fought off by that profession in the House of Commons, with the result that the chief purpose of those earlier 'petitioners', the commonwealth-

---

[84] 32 Henry VIII, c. 31; *LP* iv. 6043(3).
[85] 32 Henry VIII, c. 36; *LP* xv. 615.
[86] 32 Henry VIII, c. 38.
[87] 32 Henry VIII, c. 9; *LJ* i. 131b–133a, 135a, 148a–149a, 150a, 152a.

men working through Thomas Cromwell, were largely defeated. It may well not be without significance that the Commons did not succeed in substituting their bill until after the lord privy seal had moved from the House of Lords to the Tower.

Despite this partial and serious defeat, the government had not done too badly with its programme of law reform, though of course the achievement consisted of a number of particular details rather than a sweeping renewal of the common law. Reform by statute could hardly hope for anything else. And in the main the work had been done by operating through the House of Lords. Once again, however, the government's real intentions cannot be understood unless one takes into account bills attempted that did not pass. Some of these came up from the Commons. It was they who tried to add to the shortening of the Trinity term a similar truncation of the Easter term. This would have benefited neither practitioners nor clients, and the Lords were well advised to proceed no further with the bill.[88] The Lords also defeated a move which looks to have been too clever by half when they dropped a bill which alleged that persons without sufficient learning had been practising as counsel in lawsuits; this sounds like an attempt to buttress a monopoly already quite powerful enough.[89] Some quite promising-sounding reforms, however, were also lost in the Lords. An attempt was made to legislate for copyholds, but though the bill was cast into proper form by the solicitor-general the House did not proceed far with it.[90] Would it have done something to extend the protection of the common law to that tenure? If so, it may have been the lord chancellor, whose business would have been seriously affected, who frustrated it. A bill to safeguard orphans' goods against the wickedness of executors received but one reading; one recalls Cromwell's earlier interest in the fatherless children of London.[91] The session produced two acts concerning property rights at death, but another useful bill for the administration of the estate of a person who died intestate, though it passed the Lords, got nowhere with the Commons.[92] Lastly, there was a proposal which suggests an attack on Chancery: a bill that the causes of summons must be explained in the warrant. This really could apply only

[88] *LJ* i. 151b, 152b.   [89] Ibid.
[90] Ibid. 131a, 132a, 136a, 138b.
[91] Ibid. 139b.   [92] Ibid. 158b.

to the famous, or notorious, subpoena since the writ of tres-
pass on the case, which had also once been somewhat coy about
the specific charge alleged, had by this time developed its
particularist offspring like Assumpsit, Trover and Ejectment.
Anyway, one reading in the Lords, with the lord chancellor
presiding, ended the history of that bill.[93] The main part of the
failed bills would in this session appear to have been unofficial.

In law reform, then, the story is much as one might expect:
some very far-reaching plans based on serious analysis, some
major achievements, a good many details settled, but also some
heavy defeats and a total tally which fell well short of what had
been intended. Reforming the substance and the administration
of the law has never proved easy, however urgent the occasion;
what is clear is that Cromwell and his men made quite a considerable effort.

[93] Ibid. 146a.

7

THE ACHIEVEMENT

When one comes to consider the sum total of what was done for the common weal in the age of Thomas Cromwell, it may not appear very much. A good many people busily ferreting out the causes of distress and devising remedies, an active minister willing to give ear and himself well aware of what was wrong, a great deal of activity in preparing, piloting and passing legislation; and what does it all amount to? The large schemes of new institutions and organizations to find work for the unemployed, provide a proper enforcement of regulations, and convert the wealth of the Church to national purposes all came to little or nothing. The control of the economy was improved, but depopulating enclosure was not stopped, and though trade prospered, novel ideas of exploiting it to the national advantage and that of the navy barely survived Cromwell. The dreams of 'social engineering' turned out, as usual, to be only dreams; which, in view of some of the things proposed, was just as well, for carried into effect they might easily have become nightmares. *Utopia* should stand as a warning of what life might become if earnest reformers ever really got hold of it. The bulk of what was done did not bear much relation to the treatises of the ardent intellectuals but dealt with this or that detail of public life, in a manner long familiar. If Cromwell and his followers planned to renew the realm, it does not at first sight seem that they got very far with it.

Yet such a judgment, it seems to me, would be insufficient. In the first place, we need again to remember that the problems here studied formed but a part of the work. The largest aspect of that making over of the nation which, I suggest, Cromwell pursued as a deliberate policy concerned the Church and all that that implied: and often though the early Reformation has been studied we could still learn much more about the moral and intellectual purposes underlying the creation of the royal supremacy and the powerful evangelical movement of the 1530's. There was one side to the state's dealings with the Church which bears strongly on the social themes I have discussed, one major concern for which there has been no room in this book. Among the themes that run through both paper notions and positive action, the best use of ecclesiastical wealth stands high. Of late, the inwardness of the Dissolution has always been studied from the point of view of the monks; surprising things might emerge if that of the reformers were substituted and the matter considered in the light of social renewal. Starkey, as we have seen, wanted the wealth applied to the improvement of education, the man who dreamed up the Court of Centeners to national defence. Defence and the financial needs of the Crown are worth a study by themselves, a study which needs to weave together the practical problems of safeguarding the kingdom with the spiritual problems of the proper nature of the Church, and which would do well to avoid rash moralizing about greed and acquisitiveness. Even the taxation of this age cannot be fully understood without a grasp of the commonwealth principles upon which Cromwell's administration rested. After all, the subsidy of 1534 was the first tax levied which justified itself on the grounds of the King's services to the common weal rather than by pleading the fact or the threat of war; and a reading of the speech in support of a subsidy which Richard Morison delivered in the Parliament of 1540 (and which Cromwell helped him draft) shows how closely social policy and the need for money were intertwined.[1] I mention these further large topics only to show that the subject remains unexhausted.

No more than any other minister of the Crown was Cromwell able to concentrate all his energies on the reform of society, and far more than most he reduced the time he could give to such tasks by the variety of great causes and transformations he undertook. On top of this he was cut off in full flood; and though his impetus continued in English government, it rapidly slowed down in the hands of lesser men faced with renewed war, economic crisis, and religious revolution. Cromwell was widely known as a man who performed what he promised, and even if he did not manage in nine years to stamp out poverty or bring contentment to all sorts and conditions of men, he could lay claim to considerable achievements. The Sheep and Enclosure

[1] BM, Titus B. i, fos. 109–16 (*LP* xiv. I. 869). I hope another time to look a little more closely at this matter.

Acts at least created a proper basis for stabilizing the agrarian situation. His Poor Law, so much reduced from its first ambitious scope, still marked the real beginning of a national system of relief which was unique among the nation-states of Europe. Through all the political upheavals of the decade he managed to protect the vital cloth-trade, and he supplied quite a number of specific reforms for the advantage of commercial enterprise. The land law was revolutionized; despite the continued existence of the 'feudal incidents', the Statutes of Uses and Wills terminated the truly feudal era in its history. If he could not establish a full-scale land-register he did succeed in improving the enrolment of some deeds; and by instituting parish registers he both intended and achieved a long step towards that basis of certain information about descent which was requisite for a better order in rights of inheritance. Law reforms recorded some useful improvements in detail, and the protection of public order was well advanced by the systematic attack on unjustified asylum and evasive techniques. Later ages rightly saw the beginnings of many new starts in that decade, even though other people have been deceived by the great care taken to reform within the framework of existing concepts and institutions. Continuity and law were the wisely chosen poles which carried the banner inscribed reform and renewal.

One consequence of this determination to execute radical transformation without the outward appearance of a revolution – and let us remember that to the supporters of the old Church the outward appearance of revolution was very plain – was that the Cromwellian reforms cannot be expected to have in some obvious way put cohesive theories into executive practice. Cromwell's relations with writers and intellectuals, as we have seen, were close, but they were never those of disciple and teacher, of executor and deviser. Though himself perfectly capable of understanding the needs of the day, he wanted men who could formulate problems and their solutions, and his measures can often be shown to have grown out of particular advice. But if he could be accused, as he was by Clement Armstrong, of refusing to realize a comprehensive vision at one blow, that is only to his credit. In so far as reforms were achieved they owed as much to Cromwell's recognition of the political realities as they did to his principled search for a better commonwealth. Time and again we have seen his plans hindered or even knocked down. Occasionally it becomes plain that he wished to do things which the King, and possibly the Council, could not support: thus his failure to use that propitious time to do anything about the Church courts grew from the King's determination to rule a Church as like as possible to the pope's Church. I do not think that the full institutional survival of the medieval Church was part of Cromwell's plan, and perhaps we are a little too ready nowadays to take for granted that what happened was bound to happen. There were plenty of ideas about (not to mention foreign examples) which would have transformed the Church into no more than a ministry of the Word, without great wealth and without disciplinary powers; and the men who advanced those ideas were by no means necessarily extremists in doctrinal reform. But among the facts of social life in the 1530's was the demand for a moral rule which only the institutions of the Church could supply; and among the facts of political life were the services of Church lawyers, the power of bishops, and especially the convictions of the King. By his endeavours to turn the Church towards its tasks of preaching and moral suasion, Cromwell showed the essentially radical cast of his thinking; by his failure to put an axe to the root of the ecclesiastical organization and by his creation of the vicegerency, he showed his understanding of the practical possibilities.

However, Henry's differences from his minister did not include a different view of the common weal. The real opposition to a more extensive and radical policy of reform came, as we have seen, from Parliament. Time and again, important parts of Cromwell's programme were cut back or even down in one House or the other. If this discussion has achieved anything, it should for good and all have laid the spectre of Henry VIII's subservient Parliaments, rubberstamping all that was put before them. The interests represented in Lords and Commons both promoted legislation suitable to themselves and powerfully affected that proposed by the government. This was an entirely 'real' Parliament, perfectly capable of constructive opposition and perfectly skilled in the use of its weapons. No doubt the legislation of the royal supremacy was harder to oppose than that on enclosure or law reform, but (as we have seen) there is even a strong hint that in 1534 the two Houses may have been ahead of the King in attacking the pope. At the very least we should cease to accept standard descriptions of these Parliaments as being cowed or constrained by Henry and Cromwell into anti-papal actions unpleasing to themselves. The King's one known personal intervention in the Commons was a straightforward flop. We have for too long seen the Parliaments of the 1530's through the propaganda put out by Henry's opponents with the powerful support of the imperial ambassador. If Cromwell found it easier to legislate for the break with Rome than to pass his revolutionary Poor Law, this was at least in part because on the first he had the Parliament with him and on the second against him. No one is trying to find yet another 'age of conflict' in the history of Parliament: on the contrary, these Henrician sessions demonstrated the reality of Parliament as a meeting place of diverse views and interests, designed to produce positive results in the form of statutes. Thanks to Cromwell, the productivity of those particular Parliaments was high; thanks to his understanding of the true nature and function of Parliaments, much controversial stuff was skilfully got through and much controversial stuff was, in the face of opposition, abandoned.

Reform involves the making of new laws. But what is the virtue of burdening the statute book, especially when some of the new laws merely modified earlier legislation and were to require further attention in future? It would not have been in Cromwell's character to be content with enunciating good intentions; we need only look at the manner in which he settled the new order in the Church to understand how fully he grasped the need to make new laws work. The effectiveness of his reforms in action is something that cannot be pursued here; it would be necessary to track through yards of plea rolls and to investigate the localities in ways which the evidence extant for this period rarely permits. In any case, Cromwell's premature disappearance devolved the tasks of application upon his feebler successors. But it can be shown that he did what could immediately be done to give reality to the law.

The first important point was that the law needed to be kept in being. It does not seem to be sufficiently realized how many laws made under the early Tudors had only a limited life. One public act after another is ordered to endure to the end of the next Parliament, or for the life of the king that now is, and a good deal of the legislation so often and so solemnly discussed by legal and administrative historians had strictly speaking ceased to exist before the time which they have in review. The so-called great Statute of Retainers of 1504, for instance, died with Henry VII and was never renewed. We do not at present know how careful the courts were about lapsed statutes, and I suspect that cases could be found in which they entertained actions upon such technically defunct acts. But both by fixing such limits and by occasionally renewing an expired act, Parliament and Crown had shown that in their thinking the limited duration of some laws was intentional and real.

It is therefore, to my mind, very significant that systematic attention to expiring laws began in the Parliament of 1536, after the sizable production of important acts during the previous seven sessions many of which would have come to an end when this new Parliament dispersed. In the place of particular acts repeating or merely confirming previous legislation, we suddenly and for the first time get genuine Expiring Laws Continuance Acts. In 1536 the method was so new that it led to confusion. There were no less than five such bills, four in the Lords and one in the Commons, and the Commons' bill overlapped in one particular with one of the Lords'.[2] That the idea originated with the government is proved by the fact that the Lords' bills were all introduced by the lord chancellor; perhaps Cromwell was responsible for the Commons' bill, having for once got some lines crossed with Audley. By 1539, however, the system was working well: in that session and the next, single comprehensive Expiring Laws bills were presented in the Lords and passed without difficulty.[3] I do not know when the scrutiny of expiring acts moved formally out of the hands of the government into those of the House of Commons; at any rate, it was in Cromwell's administra-

[2] 28 Henry VIII, cc. 1 (Commons), 2, 6, 8, 9 (Lords). Cf. *LJ* i. 88a–b, 87b, 88a, 89b, 97a. The Buggery Act of 1534 was renewed in both cc. 1 and 6. According to *LJ* i. 89b, c. 6 was rejected by the Lords after the House had passed it and received it back from the Commons, a mysterious business. The act is on the book. It did cause some problems: alone of these renewal bills it was committed in the Commons and was in the end continued only to the end of the next Parliament. For a possible explanation linking this difficult passage with the 1536 Poor Law, cf. above. pp. 124–5.
[3] 31 Henry VIII, c. 7; 32 Henry VIII, c. 3. The first of these was introduced by the solicitor general; for the second the Journal omits the name of the promoter.

tion that the government first undertook to attend systematically
to the work of keeping laws in force, an activity which also made
possible the review of legislation deemed fit to lapse.

Further Cromwell showed himself well aware of the need to
press the enforcement of the laws upon those who had to apply
them in practice, and for this he used the available machinery of
proclamations. Cromwell did not fall back on proclamations for
the formulation of his policy and the creation of reforms either of
the common weal or of anything else; the opinion that Cromwell
'wanted legislation and not deliberation' and therefore preferred
proclamations to statutes should not survive even a casual study
of his employment of both.[4] When on one occasion he resorted to
a proclamation because he had failed to get an Act of Parliament,
he actually demonstrated his exceptional devotion to statute. This
was when he tried to stop the exchanges and lost the necessary
bill in the 1536 Parliament; but this was a matter in which all
law and precedent authorized action by proclamation, the method
ultimately adopted. Cromwell's first turning to Parliament thus
becomes a strikingly unusual bit of 'constitutionalism'.[5] Of the
proclamations issued during his ministry from early 1532 onwards,
only six of those concerned with the commonwealth embodied
direct action, and of these five dealt with the problems of coinage
and foreign exchange.[6] The sixth was directed against the engrossing and hoarding of bread-grain, a measure necessitated (as the
proclamation says) by a sudden rise in prices; since it prohibited
virtually all dealings in grain it was obviously a temporary
emergency measure for which statute would have been quite
unsuitable.[7] There were plenty of precedents, one as recent as
1527.[8] Even so, Cromwell had in 1532 characteristically tried for
a more lasting arrangement by means of a bill which had achieved
two readings in the Commons;[9] his experience on that occasion
may conceivably have played its part two years later in persuading him to stick to the tried methods.

So far as the common weal was concerned, Cromwell used
proclamations to apply and vary the effect of statutes. The act for

[4] J. Hurstfield, 'Was there a Tudor Despotism after all?,' *Trans. Royal
Hist. Soc.* 1967, 83–108; esp. 92–3.
[5] Above, p. 118.   [6] *TRP* i, nos. 173, 178, 180–2.
[7] Ibid. no. 151. This proclamation issued on 11 November 1534, while
Parliament was sitting.
[8] Ibid. no. 118.   [9] *LP* vi. 120(1).

meat prices (1533) met so much determined opposition that its application proved very difficult indeed; no fewer than seven proclamations were issued between 1534 and 1540, at first enforcing and later repeatedly suspending it.[10] The statutes, old and new, which set standards for the manufacture of cloth were equally hard to force upon reluctant clothmakers who claimed various disabilities, from the inadequacy of existing looms to Parliament's ignorance of particular conditions in this or that part of the realm: though proclamations ordered obedience in 1534 and 1536, Cromwell realistically gave way in September 1537 when he agreed to suspend the act of 1536 (only recently urged upon manufacturers) which, however, does not seem to have been officially promoted.[11] Three proclamations attended to the task of fixing the price of wine, as authorized by two recent statutes which had set up Council committees for the purpose.[12] The Statute of Apparel was twice suspended in 1534 for members of the royal Households, a piece of special privilege which need not surprise but hardly constitutes an act of policy.[13] In 1537 the recent act against handguns and crossbows was enforced by proclamation, and in 1538 all existing acts against unlawful games were summarized in a proclamation which appears to have been for information only.[14]

That leaves two proclamations which are rather more interesting. In February 1536, on the eve of one of the more productive sessions of Parliament, the government ordered the observation and enforcement of four kinds of commonwealth acts – for the maintenance of archery, against games, the Statute of Apparel, and the 1531 Poor Law.[15] And in March 1538 a more urgent proclamation still attempted to assure the working of those same acts with the addition of ancient statutes against rumour-mongers and the recent Statute of Sewers.[16] Cromwell wished to make it

---

[10] *TRP* i, nos. 142, 144, 148, 159, 162, 164, 193. Cf. Heinze, *Hist. Journal* xii (1969), 583–95. These suspensions incidentally suggest that statutory legislation for such purposes was more constitutional than sensible.

[11] *TRP* i, nos. 152, 166, 175; 27 Henry VIII, c. 12.

[12] Ibid. nos. 149, 170, 187.   [13] Ibid. nos. 143, 146.

[14] Ibid. nos. 171, 183.   [15] Ibid. no. 163.

[16] Ibid. no. 138, misdated there to c. 1532–3. As the editors note, the document was proclaimed in London on 6 March 1538, and there are absolutely no grounds for doubting this to be the date of the proclamation. No evidence exists for the earlier one, and proclamations were always proclaimed immediately – and not again. The result of the misdating is that

very plain that legislation was meant to be enforced, and this last proclamation is in deep earnest. 'The King's most royal majesty, who nothing more desireth than the advancement of the commonwealth of this realm' is profoundly troubled by the negligence of those officers to whom he has committed 'the cure and administration of justice and the due execution of such statutes' as are made for the general good. He therefore straitly charges 'all and singular his justices, commissioners, mayors, sheriffs, bailiffs, constables, under-constables, tithingmen, bursholders, and all other his ministers of justice...that they endeavour to do and exercise the offices, cures and authorities committed to their charge'. In this he will 'from time to time assist them, and in all their reasonable suits graciously hear them; and over that, requite their good services and diligences in his commonwealth in such wise that they shall think their travails and pains right well employed and bestowed in that behalf'. But 'high indignation and displeasure' will be visited on those failing to do their duty, and the King 'will pursue them as the very enemies of his commonwealth'. And all his majesty's subjects, 'of what estate, degree or condition soever they be', are enjoined from henceforth to 'observe and keep the said good laws and statutes', for there will be no pardon or remission of penalties for any who continue to break the law 'after this his grace's proclamation'.

Thus, in tones of fatherly care and correction, Thomas Cromwell set the standards for the commonwealth he had done so much to reform and renew. I know there is a widespread feeling that the greatness of Thomas Cromwell is something manufactured for him long after his departure. Let me therefore call to witness Dr Thomas Wilson, Queen Elizabeth's principal secretary and a man long acquainted with the inner counsels of the realm. Writing just a generation after Cromwell's death, he bitterly denounced the prevalence of usury and called for remedy. 'And shall I', he cried, 'name one who hath been in our age, and wish him now to live to cure so great a canker? Would God England had a Cromwell: I will say no more.'[17]

the editors are driven to identify the statutes listed in the proclamation as some pretty ancient ones, whereas recent ones of immediate relevance existed in 1538. The concern with rumour-mongering also belongs to the latter part of the decade (cf. *Policy and Police*, 252–3).

[17] Thomas Wilson, *Discourse on Usury* (1571), ed. R. H. Tawney (London, 1925), 182.

INDEX OF STATUTES CITED

INDEX OF FAILED BILLS

GENERAL INDEX